QUEST FOR REALITY

BOOKS BY YVOR WINTERS

The Brink of Darkness
Collected Poems
The Early Poems of Yvor Winters
Forms of Discovery
In Defense of Reason
Uncollected Essays and Reviews, Francis Murphy, Editor

QUEST
FOR
REALITY

selected
by
YVOR WINTERS
and
KENNETH FIELDS

An Anthology
of Short Poems
in English

THE **SWALLOW PRESS** INC.

CHICAGO

135652

Published by
The Swallow Press

Reprinted in 1982 by
Ohio University Press
Athens, Ohio 45701

Third Printing 1982

LIBRARY OF CONGRESS CATALOG CARD NUMBER 78-75739
ISBN 0-8040-0258-4

Throughout the world, if it were sought,
Fair words enough a man shall find;
They be good cheap, they cost right nought,
Their substance is but only wind.
　　But well to say, and so to mean,
　　That sweet accord is seldom seen.
　　　　— Sir Thomas Wyatt (c. 1503-1542)

To the Reader
I thee advise
If thou be wise
To keep thy wit
Though it be small;
'Tis rare to get
And far to fet,
'Twas ever yit
Dear'st ware of all.
　　　　— George Turberville (c. 1540-c. 1610)

CONTENTS

"ONLY AT UNCONJECTURED INTERVALS":

AN INTRODUCTION

To many readers the present anthology may well appear puzzling. Covering a period of more than 400 years, it contains only 185 poems by 48 poets.* There are a few moderately long poems, such as those by Gascoigne, Dryden, Churchill, Tuckerman, and Stevens; but most of the poems are short. The poet represented by the most poems is J. V. Cunningham, who has 16. Other poets represented by several poems are Thomas Hardy, Ben Jonson, Fulke Greville, Robert Herrick, and Emily Dickinson. A large number of poems, however, does not necessarily indicate superiority, for many of our best poets are represented by a single, extraordinary poem. Three such single poems are Sir Robert Ayton's *To an Inconstant One*, Charles Churchill's *Dedication to the Sermons*, and Alan Stephens' *Prologue: Moments in a Glade*.

It is the opinion of the editors that the two most important periods of English poetry are the sixteenth and seventeenth centuries, roughly from Sir Thomas Wyatt to John Dryden (we include 68 poems from this period), and the late nineteenth and the twentieth centuries. We include only one poem from the eighteenth century, and that is by Charles Churchill. There are no poems from the nineteenth century before those of the three Americans, Jones Very, Frederick Goddard Tuckerman, and Emily Dickinson. After Dryden, the English poets are Charles Churchill, Thomas Hardy, Robert Bridges, T. Sturge Moore, Mina Loy, Elizabeth Daryush, and Thom Gunn. For us, modern poetry is chiefly American.

---

*see Postscript

Quest for Reality should be regarded as the companion volume to Yvor Winters' *Forms of Discovery,* for the anthology attempts a definition by example of the sort of poetry which Winters has described and defended in his criticism for many years. Thus, for the editors, these 48 poets share important qualitative resemblances. The kind of poetry which we are trying to exemplify does not consist in a specific subject matter or style, but rather in a high degree of concentration which aims at understanding and revealing the particular subject as fully as possible. Today the reader is very often in search of the distinguishing mannerism of the poet—in search of accident rather than substance. And there are many poets for such readers to find, poets whose style is little more than mannerism; further, there are poets of considerable genius, such as Hopkins, Pound, Crane, and Roethke, most of whose writing is extremely mannered in various ways. But in selecting our anthology we have tried to exclude poets who seem habitually concerned with superficial mannerism, and we have tried instead to find writers whose attitude toward their art resembles Ben Jonson's, as we see it in one of his best love poems:

> And it is not always face,
> Clothes, or fortune gives the grace,
> Or the feature, or the youth;
> But the language and the truth . . .

Our best writers live fully in the knowledge that language is at once personal and public; they know that only by precisely controlling the public medium of language can they realize private experience. For each of us language is the essential intermediary between the isolated self and the world of others; rather than trammeling the mind and affections, it sets them free, giving them proper objects. And whatever else poetry may be, its medium is language—poetry is communication. Those poets who fail in their responsibilities to the public aspects of language, concentrating instead on the private or eccentric aspects, impair their ability to reveal, to themselves as well as to their readers, the reality of their experience. Such poets, however brilliant, are landlocked and are accordingly out of touch with life. As John Wild, defending ethical realism, has written, "it is at this level [of intelligible, abstract discourse] primarily that the human individual is able to escape his subjective loneliness, and to gain a direct access to the content of an alien mind." If a poet concentrates exclusively on the public nature of language, the result will usually be the cliché; if he concentrates on the private nature, the result will be obscurity. In either case, reality has eluded him, his mind is dead. The poets of this anthology, on the other hand, are consistent in one respect: they are interested in understanding and revealing, are interested in the language and the truth. They are engaged in the quest for reality.

But the quest is demanding, and the quality of writing that we most admire is not easy to attain. The best of our poets attain it in but a few poems, some in only one. Of course, one poet may aim at more or less comprehensiveness than another (in fact this distinction may be more useful than that of major and minor poetry), and the great writer who deals with limited but real subjects may enjoy extraordinary success—Herrick, Adelaide Crapsey, and William Carlos Williams are such poets. The poets, moreover, who seem most near perfection, who seem most perfectly to achieve their particular ends, are Wyatt, Jonson, Dryden, Williams, and Cunningham—writers of various degrees of profundity, sharing only in unqualified success. The reader wishing to generalize about a uniformity of specific style, subject, or temperament among our poets might first attempt a comparison of *The Lute Obeys; An Ode to Himself; No, no, poor suffering heart; The Pot of Flowers;* and *Ars Amoris.*

Besides those rare poems which are nearly flawless, there are also those which exhibit excellence but for any number of reasons do not sustain it at all times. In many ways the most problematic of these poems is Andrew Marvell's *The Garden,* a poem of very brilliant finish and written with great consistency. The main difficulty is that the paradise treated in the poem appears to be entirely private or, at best, theoretical. But Marvell's enraptured description of his paradisaic garden, as for example in the fifth stanza, is exceedingly vivid simply on a realistic level. And in the seventh stanza, the poet, by way of a simile, describes the flight of his soul as follows:

> Casting the body's vest aside,
> My soul into the boughs does glide;
> There, like a bird, it sits and sings,
> Then whets and combs its silver wings,
> And, till prepared for longer flight,
> Waves in its plumes the various light.

It may be that the bird is ornamental. Especially because it follows the sophisticated natural description· of the fifth stanza, however, it is the bird, and not the soul, that comes to life in these lines, its movements even suggested in the expert rhythms. The realities, such as they might be, of Eden and the soul tend to glide away—and to this extent the poem is imperfect—but the garden and the bird remain.

In a similar connection I should mention the poems by Henry King and F. G. Tuckerman, for in the best work of both men one nevertheless finds occasional lapses. Most of the soft writing in Tuckerman occurs in the selection called *Elegy in Six Sonnets*. Some of the sonnets are stronger than others (XVI and XVIII are especially beautiful), and one or two contain weak phrases; but the poems form a complete group and as a group are more impressive than any single poem. The subject is a somewhat complicated form of nostalgia which runs throughout his poetry; and in the *Elegy* one has the impressive treatment of a profound, lifelong preoccupation, profound because it is so articulately expressed. Even in his best poem, *The Cricket*, there is a small amount of soft writing, but it is a poem that needs no apology. And the *Sonnet XIV* from the Fifth Series seems flawless. Consider these lines:

> The gust has fallen now, and all is mute—
> Save pricking on the pane the sleety showers,
> The clock that ticks like a belated foot,
> Time's hurrying step, the twanging of the hours . . .

Likewise, in King's *The Exequy*, a poem somewhat too long, one might easily point out the weak passages, which are not many. But the best passages are as considerable as any writing in the anthology, and the whole poem is one of genuine integrity. In the following lines, the language is plain, the statement complex and exact, and, for the the reader who is listening, the syntax and the tetrameter couplet are superbly controlled.

> Mean time, thou hast her, earth: much good
> May my harm do thee. Since it stood
> With Heaven's will I might not call
> Her longer mine, I give thee all
> My short-lived right and interest
> In her, whom living I loved best:

With a most free and bounteous grief,
I give thee what I could not keep.

Like our other poets, King and Tuckerman are masters of style; in their work one sees that stylistic mastery involves an exact command of the potentialities of language—it is not simply ornament for thought. Moreover, these writers are not preoccupied with style in itself, but rather they view it as a means toward the end of understanding experience, toward the fully human apprehension of reality. The kind of perception necessary for this apprehension may be seen in Philip Pain's short poem, which deals with the difference between the concept, the isolated idea, and its human realization, the concept made real. It is a single poem of six lines; it is both remarkable and rare.

What we have said about the rareness of the first-rate poem and what we have said about the popular preference for mannerism are demonstrated clearly by the work and reputation of Thomas Hardy and of Robert Bridges. These men wrote a prodigious number of poems, most of which are flawed by characteristic weaknesses. In Hardy the weakness is a preference for the melodramatic and sentimental situation; in Bridges it is a virtually incurable predilection for stereotyped romantic diction. Yet their finest poems—and the number is relatively low in each case—overcome these faults and are not in fact representative of their total work. Insofar as Bridges is admired at all, it is usually as a late-romantic poet; his commonplace poems are the ones most frequently associated with his name. And Hardy, who is returning to popularity, is esteemed for his quaintness, for his knowledge of folk idiom, or for his dramatic situations. There are, however, few of the characteristic and popular qualities in Bridges' *Dejection* or in Hardy's "*My Spirit Will Not Haunt the Mound*," nor do more than traces of these qualities appear in our selections from their work. Hardy and Bridges remain among our very finest poets, and my remarks should in no sense be taken as apologetic. It should surprise no one that the average for success of any kind is always low; the opportunities for failure are manifold, whereas success is singular. One confronts roughly analogous situations in the work of T. Sturge Moore, E. A. Robinson, and Wallace Stevens.

With added complications, the situation obtains in the work of Emily Dickinson. On the authority of most of her 1,775 poems she is often admired for her oddness, for her distinctive "quirkiness." Now she is indeed quirky, and the quality enters into even her best poems and is responsible for much of their uniqueness; one would not have it otherwise. But, being an extremist, she often outdid herself.

To show the representative or characteristic nature of Emily Dickinson's mind in her poems, however, is not our purpose. Rather, throughout the present book, we have tried to provide the reader with the exceptional poems of exceptional poets. Doubtless, as others have done, one might illuminate persistent facts about Emily Dickinson's personality by citing lines like these (wisely omitted from *Unpublished Poems*):

> My Brain—begun to laugh—
> I mumbled—like a fool—
> And tho' 'tis Years ago—that Day—
> My Brain keeps giggling—still.

Or by citing the awkward vulgarity of the following stanza, omitted in this anthology (from *The last night that she lived*):

> We noticed smallest things,—
> Things overlooked before,
> By this great light upon our minds
> Italicized, as 't were.

In lines like the above, and even in more interesting examples like *I felt a funeral in my brain*, one has Emily Dickinson in her most mannered and, I think, her most characteristic style. It is a long way from the style of her best work.

Including her, however, was not without difficulties, the most important unquestionably being the selection of texts. For all of her poems herein, we have preferred the versions first published by Mabel Loomis Todd, Martha Dickinson Bianchi, and Alfred Leete Hampson to those of Thomas H. Johnson.* It is by now well known that the poems exist in

---

*We do not intend to invalidate what might be called the scholarly importance of Johnson's edition. But the arbitrarily selected versions to which he appends the variants should not be mistaken for the final texts; in his unannotated one-volume edition and in his selection, *Final Harvest*, the tentative and incomplete versions seem strangely to have become authoritative. (In his introduction to the 1955 variorum edition Johnson says that subsequent editions should regularize the punctuation and capitalization of the poems; however, he fails to perform this service in his own subsequent editions.) So far as Johnson does what he set out to do—that is, provide a chronology and an accurate record of all versions of the poems—his edition has limited but real usefulness. For some of the difficulties in the variorum edition see R. W. Franklin, *The Editing of Emily Dickinson: A Reconsideration*, The University of Wisconsin Press, 1967.

numerous versions and in various states of revision. For the most part Emily Dickinson did not prepare her poems for publication, and it appears impossible to determine final versions. Nor did she have what she badly needed: an intelligent critic, friend, or editor. What is needed now is an attempt to determine the best poems and the best versions. As editors, we are aware that the determination is a matter of judgment, or of taste, if you will. We are also aware of the probability, as Johnson suggests, that the earlier versions were altered by T. W. Higginson (or by Mrs. Todd and others, as Franklin suggests); but the alterations do not change the fact of Emily Dickinson's authorship. In making our choices we are not defending Higginson's intelligence. Neither do we think it necessary to suppose that he made the changes, if indeed he made them, in the interests of the genteel critical standards of his day; it may simply have been a matter of tact. He appears to have guessed that something needed to be done if those strange poems were to survive. In view of the widespread acceptance of Johnson's texts, it should be clear that something must be done today. It ought to make little difference who finished the nine poems that we have chosen (in fact the textual changes are few); the poems are still hers, and they are among the most singular poems in our collection.

I should like to quote the relevant lines from one of her best and most famous poems, *There's a certain slant of light*; this is the version we use:

> There's a certain slant of light,
> On winter afternoons,
> That oppresses, like the weight
> Of cathedral tunes.
>   *   *   *
> None may teach it anything,
> 'Tis the seal, despair,—
> An imperial affliction
> Sent us of the air.

One should like to find it unnecessary to say that this version is clearly superior to the "unaltered" version given by Johnson, though the differences may at first appear slight—"Winter afternoons" in the second line; "Heft" for "weight," and "Any" for "anything." The Johnson version, although perhaps an illustration of Emily Dickinson's cranky sort of genius, cannot stand as it is. In terms I have already used, the poem exploits the personal and eccentric aspects of language to the detriment of the public or general aspects, and consequently it is badly marred. Johnson's version (which may, in fairness, have been Emily Dickinson's only version) is almost universally accepted. It is possible, though, that its appeal results from its superficial and obviously distinctive features: they are extremely easy to identify and easy to discuss. Entire lectures, one imagines, might be devoted to "oppresses like the Heft" and "None may teach it Any," whereas the less eccentric version might leave many people with nothing to say about it. Nevertheless, it is the truer poem, its virtues are more real and they are harder to distinguish. It touches more of life. The two versions of the poem illustrate something of the significance of James Baldwin's penetrating observation that the writer works "in the disastrously explicit medium of language."

Such triumphs of language are always rare and necessarily emerge from a great deal of unsuccessful writing. And if the exceptional poem is a rare occasion, so too is its appreciation. It is possible that the reader who cannot appreciate the reasons for our selection of the Dickinson texts, and who prefers Johnson's versions, will have some difficulty perceiving the reasons for our other choices as well.

As I have said earlier, *Quest for Reality* is a companion volume to *Forms of Discovery*; to understand the anthology properly one should be familiar with the critical book. In *Forms* many of the poems of this anthology are fully discussed, and one gets a good deal of the theory and history of English poetry in addition. Moreover, the book deals with a number of important poems not included here.

Finally, the anthology should be read with attention from beginning to end—the reader will miss its coherence if he examines a poem here and there, or merely scans the table of contents. We have tried to be definitive, and we trust that reading the anthology will be educational. We hope very much that the book will teach, and yet it is not a *teaching anthology* in the usual sense. There are many additional poems that one would wish to include if one were using it solely as a textbook. On the other hand, we can imagine a course, or courses, which would use the book as a central text—in fact, Yvor Winters taught most of these poems for many years. Furthermore, we offer the teacher and the student 185 excellent poems, in our opinion the most remarkable poems in English. And most of them are not easily available elsewhere. Seeing them in juxtaposition can be startling and illuminating —it has been so for us. For the standard historical choices, which no course should ignore, the teacher can supplement *Quest for Reality* with an inexpensive paperback anthology. Almost any current anthology will do.

Kenneth Fields

Postscript.

Before his death in January of this year Yvor Winters saw the publication of his *Early Poems* (1966), his great critical book, *Forms of Discovery* (1967), and the brief tribute to his late publisher, Alan Swallow *(Southern Review,* Summer 1967); and he saw the completed manuscript of this anthology. He had finished his work. Although he is best known as a critic, his highest achievements are his poems, twelve of which I now include in *Quest for Reality*, not by way of tribute, not in his memory, but solely because of their excellence. He did not see fit to include his own poems because he had grown to dislike this common editorial practice. No longer an editor of this anthology, however, he may now take his place with the poets of the world, with "the dead alive and busy."

K. F.
Feb. 4, 1968

SIR THOMAS WYATT   (c. 1503-1542)

Remembrance

They flee from me, that sometime did me seek
  With naked foot, stalking in my chamber.
I have seen them gentle, tame, and meek,
  That now are wild, and do not remember
  That sometime they put themselves in danger
    To take bread at my hand; and now they range
    Busily seeking with a continual change.

Thanked be fortune it hath been otherwise
  Twenty times better; but once, in special,
In thin array, after a pleasant guise,
  When her loose gown from her shoulders did fall,
  And she me caught in her arms long and small,
    Therewith all sweetly did me kiss
    And softly said, 'Dear heart how like you this?'

It was no dream; I lay broad waking:
  But all is turned, through my gentleness,
Into a strange fashion of forsaking;
  And I have leave to go of her goodness,
  And she also to use newfangleness.
    But since that I so kindly am served,
    I would fain know what she hath deserved.

Tagus, Farewell

Tagus, farewell, that westward with thy streams
  Turns up the grains of gold already tried;
For I with spur and sail go seek the Thames,
  Gainward the sun that showeth her wealthy pride,
And to the town that Brutus sought by dreams,
  Like bended moon, doth lean her lusty side.
    My king, my country, alone for whom I live,
    Of mighty love the wings for this me give.

To His Lute

My lute, awake! perform the last
Labor that thou and I shall waste,
   And end that I have now begun;
And when this song is sung and past,
   My lute, be still, for I have done.

As to be heard where ear is none,
As lead to grave in marble stone,
   My song may pierce her heart as soon.
Should we then sigh, or sing, or moan?
   No, no, my lute, for I have done.

The rocks do not so cruelly
Repulse the waves continually,
   As she my suit and affection;
So that I am past remedy,
   Whereby my lute and I have done.

Proud of the spoil that thou hast got
Of simple hearts through love's shot,
   By whom, unkind, thou hast them won,
Think not he hath his bow forgot,
   Although my lute and I have done.

Vengeance shall fall on thy disdain,
That makest but game on earnest pain;
   Think not alone under the sun
Unquit to cause thy lovers plain,
   Although my lute and I have done.

Perchance thee lie withered and old,
The winter nights that are so cold,
   Plaining in vain unto the moon;
Thy wishes then dare not be told.
   Care then who list, for I have done.

And then may chance thee to repent
The time that thou hast lost and spent
   To cause thy lovers sigh and swoon;
Then shalt thou know beauty but lent,
   And wish and want as I have done.

Now cease, my lute! this is the last
Labor that thou and I shall waste,
   And ended is that we begun;
Now is this song both sung and past.
   My lute, be still, for I have done.

The Lute Obeys

Blame not my lute! for he must sound
  Of these and that as liketh me;
For lack of wit the lute is bound
  To give such tunes as pleaseth me.
Though my songs be somewhat strange,
And speaks such words as touch thy change,
      Blame not my lute!

My lute, alas! doth not offend,
  Though that perforce he must agree
To sound such tunes as I intend
  To sing to them that heareth me;
Then though my songs be somewhat plain,
And toucheth some that use to feign,
      Blame not my lute!

My lute and strings may not deny,
  But as I strike they must obey;
Break not them then so wrongfully,
  But wreak thyself some wiser way;
And though the songs which I indite
Do quit thy change with rightful spite,
      Blame not my lute!

Spite asketh spite, and changing change,
  And falsed faith must needs be known;
The fault so great, the case so strange,
  Of right it must abroad be blown;
Then since that by thine own desert
My songs do tell how true thou art,
      Blame not my lute!

Blame but thy self that hast misdone
  And well deserved to have blame;
Change thou thy way, so evil begone,
  And then my lute shall sound that same;
But if till then my fingers play
By thy desert their wonted way,
      Blame not my lute!

Farewell, unknown! for though thou break
  My strings in spite with great disdain,
Yet have I found out, for thy sake,
  Strings for to string my lute again.
And if, perchance, this silly rhyme
Do make thee blush at any time,
      Blame not my lute!

Varium et Mutabile

Is it possible
  That so high debate,
  So sharp, so sore, and of such rate,
  Should end so soon that was begun so late?
Is it possible?

Is it possible
  So cruel intent,
  So hasty heat and so soon spent,
  From love to hate, and thence for to relent?
Is it possible?

Is it possible
  That any may find
  Within one heart so diverse mind,
  To change or turn as weather and wind?
Is it possible?

Is it possible
  To spy it in an eye
  That turns as oft as chance on die,
  The truth whereof can any try?
Is it possible?

It is possible
  For to turn so oft
  To bring that lowest that was most aloft,
  And to fall highest, yet to light soft.
It is possible.

All is possible,
  Who so list believe;
  Trust therefore first, and after preve,
  As men wed ladies by license and leave,
All is possible.

It Was My Choice

It was my choice, it was no chance
   That brought my heart in others' hold,
Whereby it hath had sufferance
   Longer, perdie, than Reason would;
Since I it bound where it was free,
   Methinks, iwis, of right it should
     Accepted be.

Accepted be without refuse,
   Unless that Fortune have the power
All right of love for to abuse;
   For, as they say, one happy hour
May more prevail than right or might;
   If fortune then list for to lour,
     What vaileth right?

What vaileth right if this be true?
   Then trust to chance and go by guess;
Then who so loveth may well go sue
   Uncertain Hope for his redress.
Yet some would say assuredly
   Thou mayst appeal for thy release
     To fantasy.

To fantasy pertains to choose:
   All this I know, for fantasy
First unto love did me induce;
   But yet I know as steadfastly
That if love have no faster knot,
   So nice a choice slips suddenly:
     It lasteth not.

It lasteth not that stands by change.
   Fancy doth change; fortune is frail;
Both these to please the way is strange.
   Therefore me thinks best to prevail:
There is no way that is so just
   As truth to lead, through t'other **fail**,
     And thereto trust.

THOMAS, LORD VAUX   (1510-1556)

Content

When all is done and said, in the end thus shall you find,
He most of all doth bathe in bliss that hath a quiet mind;
And, clear from worldly cares, to deem can be content
The sweetest time in all his life in thinking to be spent.

The body subject is to fickle Fortune's power,
And to a million of mishaps is casual every hour;
And death in time doth change it to a clod of clay;
Whenas the mind, which is divine, runs never to decay.

Companion none is like unto the mind alone,
For many have been harmed by speech; through thinking,
   few or none.
Fear oftentimes restraineth words, but makes not thoughts
   to cease;
And he speaks best that hath the skill when for to hold
   his peace.

Our wealth leaves us at death, our kinsmen at the grave;
But virtues of the mind unto the heavens with us we have.
Wherefore, for virtue's sake, I can be well content
The sweetest time of all my life to deem in thinking spent.

GEORGE GASCOIGNE   (c. 1525-1577)

The Lullaby of a Lover

Sing lullaby, as women do,
Wherewith they bring their babes to rest,
And lullaby can I sing too,
As womanly as can the best.
With lullaby they still the child,
And if I be not much beguiled,
Full many wanton babes have I,
Which must be stilled with lullaby.

First lullaby my youthful years,
It is now time to go to bed,
For crooked age and hoary hairs,
Have won the haven within my head:
With lullaby then youth be still,
With lullaby content thy will,
Since courage quails, and comes behind,
Go sleep, and so beguile thy mind.

Next lullaby my gazing eyes,
Which wonted were to glance apace.
For every glass may now suffice,
To show the furrows in my face:
With lullaby then wink awhile,
With lullaby your looks beguile:
Let no fair face, nor beauty bright,
Entice you eft with vain delight.

And lullaby my wanton will,
Let reasons rule, now reign thy thought,
Since all too late I find by skill,
How dear I have thy fancies bought:
With lullaby now take thine ease,
With lullaby thy doubts appease:
For trust to this, if thou be still,
My body shall obey thy will.

Eke lullaby my loving boy,
My little Robin take thy rest,
Since age is cold, and nothing coy,
Keep close thy coin, for so is best:
With lullaby be thou content,
With lullaby thy lusts relent,
Let others pay which hath mo pence,
Thou art too poor for such expense.

Thus lullaby my youth, mine eyes,
My will, my ware, and all that was,
I can no mo delays devise,
But welcome pain, let pleasure pass:
With lullaby now take your leave,
With lullaby your dreams deceive,
And when you rise with waking eye,
Remember then this lullaby.

Gascoigne's Woodmanship

My worthy Lord, I pray you wonder not,
To see your woodman shoot so oft awry,
Nor that he stands amazed like a sot,
And lets the harmless deer (unhurt) go by.
Or if he strike a Doe which is but carren,
Laugh not good Lord, but favor such a fault,
Take will in worth, he would fain hit the barren,
But though his heart be good, his hap is naught:
And therefore now I crave your Lordship's leave,
To tell you plain what is the cause of this:
First if it please your honor to perceive,
What makes your woodman shoot so oft amiss,
Believe me Lord the case is nothing strange,
He shoots awry almost at every mark,
His eyes have been so used for to range,
That now God knows they be both dim and dark.
For proof he bears the note of folly now,
Who shot sometimes to hit Philosophy,
And ask you why? forsooth I make avow.
Because his wanton wits went all awry.
Next that, he shot to be a man of law,
And spent some time with learned Littleton,
Yet in the end, he proved but a daw,
For law was dark and he had quickly done.
Then could he with Fitzherbert such a brain,
As Tully had, to write the law by art,
So that with pleasure, or with little pain,
He might perhaps, have caught a truant's part.
But all too late, he most misliked the thing,
Which most might help to guide his arrow straight:
He winked wrong, and so let slip the string,
Which cast him wide, for all his quaint conceit.
From thence he shot to catch a courtly grace,
And thought even there to wield the world at will,
But out alas he much mistook the place,
And shot awry at every rover still.
The blazing baits which draw the gazing eye,
Unfeathered there his first affection,
No wonder then although he shot awry,
Wanting the feathers of discretion.

Yet more than them, the marks of dignity,
He much mistook and shot the wronger way,
Thinking the purse of prodigality,
Had been best mean to purchase such a prey.
He thought the flattering face which fleareth still,
Had been full fraught with all fidelity,
And that such words as courtiers use at will,
Could not have varied from the verity.
But when his bonnet buttoned with gold,
His comely cape beguarded all with gay,
His bombast hose, with linings manifold,
His knit silk stocks and all his quaint array,
Had picked his purse of all the Peter pence,
Which might have paid for his promotion,
Then (all too late) he found that light expense,
Had quite quenched out the court's devotion.
So that since then the taste of misery,
Hath been always full bitter in his bit,
And why? forsooth because he shot awry,
Mistaking still the marks which others hit.
But now behold what mark the man doth find,
He shoots to be a soldier in his age,
Mistrusting all the virtues of the mind,
He trusts the power of his personage.
As though long limbs led by a lusty heart,
Might yet suffice to make him rich again,
But Flushing frays have taught him such a part,
That now he thinks the wars yield no such gain.
And sure I fear, unless your lordship deign,
To train him yet into some better trade,
It will be long before he hit the vein,
Whereby he may a richer man be made.
He cannot climb as other catchers can,
To lead a charge before himself be led,
He cannot spoil the simple sakeless man,
Which is content to feed him with his bread.
He cannot pinch the painful soldier's pay,
And shear him out his share in ragged sheets,
He cannot stoop to take a greedy prey
Upon his fellows groveling in the streets.
He cannot pull the spoil from such as pill,
And seem full angry at such foul offense,
Although the gain content his greedy will,
Under the cloak of contrary pretence:

And now adays, the man that shoots not so,
May shoot amiss, even as your Woodman doth:
But then you marvel why I let them go,
And never shoot, but say farewell forsooth:
Alas my Lord, while I do muse hereon,
And call to mind my youthful years misspent,
They give me such a bone to gnaw upon,
That all my senses are in silence pent.
My mind is rapt in contemplation,
Wherein my dazzled eyes only behold,
The black hour of my constellation,
Which framed me so luckless on the mold:
Yet therewithall I can not but confess,
That vain presumption makes my heart to swell,
For thus I think, not all the world (I guess)
Shoots bet than I, nay some shoot not so well.
In *Aristotle* somewhat did I learn,
To guide my manners all by comeliness,
And *Tully* taught me somewhat to discern
Between sweet speech and barbarous rudeness.
Old *Parkins, Rastall,* and *Dan Bracten's* books
Did lend me somewhat of the lawless Law,
The crafty Courtiers with their guileful looks,
Must needs put some experience in my maw:
Yet can not these with many masteries mo,
Make me shoot straight at any gainful prick,
Where some that never handled such a bow,
Can hit the white, or touch it near the quick,
Who can nor speak, nor write in pleasant wise,
Nor lead their life by *Aristotle's* rule,
Nor argue well on questions that arise,
Nor plead a case more than my Lord Mayor's mule,
Yet can they hit the marks that I do miss,
And win the mean which may the man maintain.
Now when my mind doth mumble upon this,
No wonder then although I pine for pain:
And whiles mine eyes behold this mirror thus,
The herd goeth by, and farewell gentle does.
So that your Lordship quickly may discuss
What blinds mine eyes so oft (as I suppose).
But since my Muse can to my Lord rehearse
What makes me miss, and why I do not shoot,
Let me imagine in this worthless verse,
If right before me, at my standing's foot

There stood a Doe, and I should strike her dead,
And then she prove a carrion carcass too,
What figure might I find within my head,
To 'scuse the rage which ruled me so to do?
Some might interpret by plain paraphrase,
That lack of skill or fortune led the chance,
But I must otherwise expound the case;
I say *Jehovah* did this Doe advance,
And make her bold to stand before me so,
Till I had thrust mine arrow to her heart,
That by the sudden of her overthrow,
I might endeavor to amend my part,
And turn mine eyes that they no more behold,
Such guileful marks as seem more than they be:
And though they glister outwardly like gold,
Are inwardly but brass, as men may see:
And when I see the milk hang in her teat,
Me thinks it saith, old babe now learn to suck
Who in thy youth couldst never learn the feat
To hit the whites which live with all good luck.
Thus have I told my Lord, (God grant in season)
A tedious tale in rime, but little reason.

The Constancy of a Lover

That selfsame tongue which first did thee entreat
To link thy liking with my lucky love:
That trusty tongue must now these words repeat,
I love thee still, my fancy cannot move.
That dreadless heart which durst attempt the thought
To win thy will with mine for to consent,
Maintains that vow which love in me first wrought,
I love thee still, and never shall repent.
That happy hand which hardily did touch,
Thy tender body to my deep delight:
Shall serve with sword to prove my passion such
As loves thee still, much more than it can write.
Thus love I still with tongue, hand, heart and all,
And when I change, let vengeance on me fall.

SIR WALTER RALEIGH   (c. 1552-1618)

The Lie

Go, soul, the body's guest,
  Upon a thankless arrant;
Fear not to touch the best;
  The truth shall be thy warrant.
    Go, since I needs must die,
    And give the world the lie.

Say to the court, it glows
  And shines like rotten wood;
Say to the church, it shows
  What's good, and doth no good:
    If church and court reply,
    Then give them both the lie.

Tell potentates, they live
  Acting by others' action,
Not loved unless they give,
  Not strong but by their faction:
    If potentates reply,
    Give potentates the lie.

Tell men of high condition
  That manage the estate,
Their purpose is ambition,
  Their practice only hate:
    And if they once reply,
    Then give them all the lie.

Tell them that brave it most,
  They beg for more by spending,
Who, in their greatest cost,
  Seek nothing but commending:
    And if they make reply,
    Then give them all the lie.

Tell zeal it wants devotion;
  Tell love it is but lust;
Tell time it is but motion;
  Tell flesh it is but dust:
    And wish them not reply,
    For thou must give the lie.

Tell age it daily wasteth;
  Tell honor how it alters;
Tell beauty how she blasteth;
  Tell favor how it falters:
    And as they shall reply,
    Give every one the lie.

Tell wit how much it wrangles
  In tickle points of niceness;
Tell wisdom she entangles
  Herself in over-wiseness:
    And when they do reply,
    Straight give them both the lie.

Tell physic of her boldness;
  Tell skill it is prevention;
Tell charity of coldness;
  Tell law it is contention:
    And as they do reply,
    Straight give them both the lie.

Tell fortune of her blindness;
  Tell nature of decay;
Tell friendship of unkindness;
  Tell justice of delay:
    And if they will reply,
    Then give them all the lie.

Tell arts they have no soundness,
  But vary by esteeming;
Tell schools they want profoundness,
  And stand too much on seeming:
    If arts and schools reply,
    Give arts and schools the lie.

Tell faith it's fled the city;
  Tell how the country erreth;
Tell, manhood shakes off pity;
  Tell, virtue least preferreth:
    And if they do reply,
    Spare not to give the lie.

So when thou hast, as I
    Commanded thee, done blabbing,
Although to give the lie
    Deserves no less than stabbing,
        Stab at thee he that will,
        No stab the soul can kill.

On the Life of Man

What is our life? A play of passion,
Our mirth the music of division.
Our mothers' wombs the tiring-houses be,
Where we are dressed for this short comedy.
Heaven the judicious sharp spectator is,
That sits and marks still who doth act amiss.
Our graves that hide us from the searching sun
Are like drawn curtains when the play is done.
Thus march we, playing, to our latest rest,
Only we die in earnest, that's no jest.

SIR PHILIP SIDNEY   (1554-1586)

Who Hath His Fancy Pleased

Who hath his fancy pleased
  With fruits of happy sight,
Let here his eyes be raised
  On Nature's sweetest light;
A light which doth dissever
  And yet unite the eyes;
A light which, dying never,
  Is cause the looker dies.

She never dies, but lasteth
  In life of lover's heart;
He ever dies that wasteth
  In love his chiefest part.
Thus is her life still guarded
  In never-dying faith;
Thus is his death rewarded,
  Since she lives in his death.

Look, then, and die; the pleasure
  Doth answer well the pain;
Small loss of mortal treasure
  Who may immortal gain.
Immortal be her graces,
  Immortal is her mind;
They, fit for heavenly places;
  This, heaven in it doth bind.

But eyes these beauties see not,
  Nor sense that grace descries;
Yet eyes deprived be not
  From sight of her fair eyes;
Which as of inward glory
  They are the outward seal,
So may they live still sorry,
  Which die not in that weal.

But who hath fancies pleased
  With fruits of happy sight,
Let here his eyes be raised
  On Nature's sweetest light!

FULKE GREVILLE, LORD BROOKE   (1554-1628)

Sonnet XXII

I with whose colors *Myra* dressed her head,
I, that wore posies of her own hand making,
I, that mine own name in the chimneys read
By *Myra* finely wrought ere I was waking:
    Must I look on, in hope time coming may
    With change bring back my turn again to play?

I, that on Sunday at the Church-stile found,
A Garland sweet, with true-love knots in flowers,
Which I to wear about mine arm was bound,
That each of us might know that all was ours:
    Must I now lead an idle life in wishes?
    And follow *Cupid* for his loaves, and fishes?

I, that did wear the ring her Mother left,
I, for whose love she gloried to be blamed,
I, with whose eyes her eyes committed theft,
I, who did make her blush when I was named;
    Must I lose ring, flowers, blush, theft and go naked,
    Watching with sighs, till dead love be awaked?

I, that when drowsy *Argus* fell asleep,
Like Jealousy o'rewatched with desire,
Was even warned modesty to keep,
While her breath, speaking, kindled Nature's fire:
    Must I look on a-cold, while others warm them?
    Do *Vulcans* brothers in such fine nets arm them?

Was it for this that I might *Myra* see
Washing the water with her beauties, white?
Yet would she never write her love to me;
Thinks wit of change while thoughts are in delight?
    Mad Girls must safely love, as they may leave,
    No man can print a kiss, lines may deceive.

Sonnet LVI

All my senses, like Beacon's flame,
Gave *Alarum* to desire
To take arms in *Cynthia's* name,
And set all my thoughts on fire:
Furies wit persuaded me,
Happy love was hazard's hire,
Cupid did best shoot and see
In the night where smooth is fair;
Up I start believing well
To see if *Cynthia* were awake;
Wonders I saw, who can tell?
And thus unto myself I spake;
Sweet God *Cupid* where am I,
That by pale *Diana's* light:
Such rich beauties do espy,
As harm our senses with delight?
Am I born up to the skies?
See where Jove and Venus shine,
Showing in her heavenly eyes
That desire is divine:
Look where lies the Milken way,
Way unto that dainty throne,
Where while all the Gods would play,
Vulcan thinks to dwell alone.
I gave reins to this conceit,
Hope went on the wheel of lust:
Fancy's scales are false of weight,
Thoughts take thought that go of trust,
I stepped forth to touch the sky,
I a God by *Cupid* dreams,
Cynthia who did naked lie,
Runs away like silver streams;
Leaving hollow banks behind,
Who can neither forward move,
Nor if rivers be unkind,
Turn away or leave to love.
There stand I, like *Arctic* pole,
Where *Sol* passeth o're the *line*,
Mourning my benighted soul,
Which so loseth light divine.
There stand I like Men that preach
From the Execution place,

At their death content to teach
All the world with their disgrace:
He that lets his *Cynthia* lie,
Naked on a bed of play,
To say prayers ere she die,
Teacheth time to run away:
Let no Love-desiring heart,
In the Stars go seek his fate,
Love is only Nature's art,
Wonder hinders Love and Hate.
   None can well behold with eyes,
   But what underneath him lies.

Sonnet LXXXIV

Farewell sweet Boy, complain not of my truth;
Thy Mother loved thee not with more devotion;
For to thy Boy's play I gave all my youth,
Young Master, I did hope for your promotion.

While some sought Honors, Princes' thoughts observing,
Many wooed *Fame, the child of pain and anguish,*
Others judged inward good a chief deserving,
I in thy wanton Visions joyed to languish.

I bowed not to thy image for succession,
Nor bound thy bow to shoot reformed kindness,
Thy plays of hope and fear were my confession,
The spectacles to my life was thy blindness;
   But *Cupid* now farewell, I will go play me,
   With thoughts that please me less, and less betray me.

Sonnet LXXXVI

The Earth with thunder torn, with fire blasted,
With waters drowned, with windy palsy shaken
Cannot for this with heaven be distasted,
Since thunder, rain and winds from earth are taken:
Man torn with Love, with inward furies blasted,
Drowned with despair, with fleshly lustings shaken,
Cannot for this with heaven be distasted,
Love, fury, lustings out of man are taken.
Then Man, endure thy self, those clouds will vanish;
Life is a Top which whipping Sorrow driveth;
Wisdom must bear what our flesh cannot banish,
The humble lead, the stubborn bootless striveth:
   Or Man, forsake thy self, to heaven turn thee,
   Her flames enlighten Nature, never burn thee.

Sonnet LXXXVIII

Man, dream no more of curious mysteries,
As what was here before the world was made,
The first Man's life, the state of Paradise,
Where heaven is, or hell's eternal shade,
   For God's works are like him, all infinite;
   And curious search, but crafty sin's delight.

The Flood that did, and dreadful Fire that shall,
Drown, and burn up the malice of the earth,
The divers tongues, and Babylon's down-fall,
Are nothing to the man's renewed birth;
   First, let the Law plough up thy wicked heart,
   That Christ may come, and all these types depart.

When thou hast swept the house that all is clear,
When thou the dust hast shaken from thy feet,
When God's All-might doth in thy flesh appear,
Then Seas with streams above thy sky do meet;
   For Goodness only doth God comprehend,
   Knows what was first, and what shall be the end.

Sonnet XCVIII

Wrapped up, O Lord, in man's degeneration;
The glories of thy truth, thy joys eternal,
Reflect upon my soul dark desolation,
And ugly prospects o'er the sprites infernal.
   Lord, I have sinned, and mine iniquity,
   Deserves this hell; yet Lord deliver me.

Thy power and mercy never comprehended,
Rest lively imaged in my Conscience wounded;
Mercy to grace, and power to fear extended,
Both infinite, and I in both confounded;
   Lord, I have sinned, and mine iniquity,
   Deserves this hell, yet Lord deliver me.

If from this depth of sin, this hellish grave,
And fatal absence from my Saviour's glory,
I could implore his mercy, who can save,
And for my sin, not pains of sin, be sorry:
   Lord, from this horror of iniquity,
   And hellish grave, thou wouldst deliver me.

Sonnet XCIX

Down in the depth of mine iniquity,
That ugly center of infernal spirits;
Where each sin feels her own deformity,
In these peculiar torments she inherits,
   Deprived of human graces, and divine,
   Even there appears this *saving God* of mine.

And in this fatal mirror of transgression,
Shows man as fruit of his degeneration,
The error's ugly infinite impression,
Which bears the faithless down to desperation;
   Deprived of human graces and divine,
   Even there appears this *saving God* of mine.

In power and truth, Almighty and eternal,
Which on the sin reflects strange desolation,
With glory scourging all the Sprites infernal,
And uncreated hell with unprivation;
   Deprived of human graces, not divine,
   Even there appears this *saving God* of mine.

For on this spritual Cross condemned lying,
To pains infernal by eternal doom,
I see my Saviour for the same sins dying,
And from that hell I feared, to free me, come;
   Deprived of human graces, not divine,
   Thus hath his death raised up this soul of mine.

Sonnet C

In Night when colors all to black are cast,
Distinction lost, or gone down with the light;
The eye a watch to inward senses placed,
Not seeing, yet still having power of sight,

Gives vain *Alarums* to the inward sense,
Where fear stirred up with witty tyranny,
Confounds all powers, and through self-offence,
Doth forge and raise impossibility:

Such as in thick depriving darknesses,
Proper reflections of the error be,
And images of self-confusednesses,
Which hurt imaginations only see;
   And from this nothing seen, tells news of devils,
   Which but expressions be of inward evils.

Sonnet CIX

Sion lies waste, and thy *Jerusalem,*
O Lord, is fallen to utter desolation,
Against thy Prophets, and thy holy men,
The sin hath wrought a fatal combination,
　　Profaned thy name, thy worship overthrown,
　　And made thee living Lord, a God unknown.

Thy powerful laws, thy wonders of creation,
Thy Word incarnate, glorious heaven, dark hell,
Lie shadowed under Man's degeneration,
Thy Christ still crucified for doing well,
　　Impiety, O Lord, sits on thy throne,
　　Which makes thee living Light, a God unknown.

Man's superstition hath thy truths entombed,
His Atheism again her pomps defaceth,
That sensual unsatiable vast womb
Of thy seen Church, thy unseen Church disgraceth;
　　There lives no truth with them that seem thine own,
　　Which makes thee living Lord, a God unknown.

Yet unto thee, Lord, (mirror of transgression)
We, who for earthly Idols, have forsaken
Thy heavenly Image (sinless pure impression)
And so in nets of vanity lie taken,
　　All desolate implore that to thine own,
　　Lord, thou no longer live a God unknown.

Yet Lord let *Israel's* plagues not be eternal,
Nor sin forever cloud thy sacred Mountains,
Nor with false flames spiritual but infernal,
Dry up thy mercy's ever-springing fountains,
　　Rather, sweet *Jesus*, fill up time and come,
　　To yield the sin her everlasting doom.

MARK ALEXANDER BOYD   (1563-1601)

Fra bank to bank

Fra bank to bank, fra wood to wood I rin,
   Ourhailit with my feeble fantasie;
   Like til a leaf that fallis from a tree,
Or til a reed ourblawin with the win.

Twa gods guides me: the ane of tham is blin,
   Yea and a bairn brocht up in vanitie;
   The next a wife ingenrit of the sea,
And lichter nor a dauphin with her fin.

Unhappy is the man for evermair
   That tills the sand and sawis in the air;
   But twice unhappier is he, I lairn,
That feidis in his hairt a mad desire,
And follows on a woman throw the fire,
   Led by a blind and teachit by a bairn.

JOHN DOWLAND   (c. 1563-c. 1626)

Fine knacks for ladies

Fine knacks for ladies, cheap, choice, brave and new!
Good pennyworths! but money cannot move.
I keep a fair but for the fair to view;
A begger may be liberal of love.
Though all my wares be trash, the heart is true.

Great gifts are guiles and look for gifts again;
My trifles come as treasures from my mind.
It is a precious jewel to be plain;
Sometimes in shell the Orient's pearls we find.
Of others take a sheaf, of me a grain.

Within this pack pins, points, laces, and gloves,
And divers toys fitting a country fair.
But my heart lives, where duty serves and loves,
Turtles and twins, court's brood, a heavenly pair.
Happy the heart that thinks of no removes.

Flow not so fast

Flow not so fast, ye fountains;
What needeth all this haste?
Swell not above your mountains,
Nor spend your time in waste.
Gentle springs, freshly your salt tears
Must still fall dropping from their spheres.

Weep they apace whom Reason
Or lingering Time can ease.
My sorrow can no Season,
Nor aught besides, appease.
Gentle springs, freshly your salt tears
Must still fall dropping from their spheres.

Time can abate the terror
Of every common pain;
But common grief is error,
True grief will still remain.
Gentle springs, freshly your salt tears
Must still fall dropping from their spheres.

WILLIAM SHAKESPEARE   (1564-1616)

Sonnet LXXIII

That time of year thou mayst in me behold
When yellow leaves, or none, or few, do hang
Upon those boughs which shake against the cold,
Bare ruined choirs where late the sweet birds sang.
In me thou see'st the twilight of such day
As after sunset fadeth in the west,
Which by and by black night doth take away,
Death's second self, that seals up all in rest.
In me thou see'st the glowing of such fire,
That on the ashes of his youth doth lie
As the deathbed whereon it must expire,
Consumed with that which it was nourished by.
   This thou perceiv'st, which makes thy love more strong,
    To love that well which thou must leave ere long.

Sonnet LXXVII

Thy glass will show thee how thy beauties wear,
Thy dial how thy precious minutes waste.
The vacant leaves thy mind's imprint will bear,
And of this book this learning mayst thou taste.
The wrinkles which thy glass will truly show
Of mouthed graves will give thee memory.
Thou by thy dial's shady stealth mayst know
Time's thievish progress to eternity.
Look, what thy memory cannot contain
Commit to these waste blanks, and thou shalt find
Those children nursed, delivered from thy brain,
To take a new acquaintance of thy mind.
   These offices, so oft as thou wilt look,
    Shall profit thee and much enrich thy book.

Sonnet LXXXVII

Farewell! Thou art too dear for my possessing,
And like enough thou know'st thy estimate.
The charter of thy worth gives thee releasing,
My bonds in thee are all determinate.
For how do I hold thee but by thy granting?
And for that riches where is my deserving?
The cause of this fair gift in me is wanting,
And so my patent back again is swerving.
Thyself thou gav'st, thy own worth then not knowing,
Or me, to whom thou gav'st it, else mistaking.
So thy great gift, upon misprision growing,
Comes home again, on better judgment making.
    Thus have I had thee, as a dream doth flatter,
    In sleep a king, but waking no such matter.

Sonnet CXXIX

The expense of spirit in a waste of shame
Is lust in action, and till action, lust
Is perjured, murderous, bloody, full of blame,
Savage, extreme, rude, cruel, not to trust,
Enjoyed no sooner but despised straight,
Past reason hunted, and no sooner had,
Past reason hated, as a swallowed bait,
On purpose laid to make the taker mad.
Mad in pursuit, and in possession so,
Had, having, and in quest to have, extreme,
A bliss in proof, and proved, a very woe.
Before, a joy proposed, behind, a dream.
    All this the world well knows, yet none knows well
    To shun the Heaven that leads men to this Hell.

from *Hamlet*

How should I your truelove know

How should I your truelove know
   From another one?
By his cockle hat and staff
   And his sandal shoon.

He is dead and gone, lady,
   He is dead and gone,
At his head a grass-green turf,
   At his heels a stone.

White his shroud as the mountain snow
   Larded with sweet flowers,
Which bewept to the grave did go
   With truelove showers.

from *Cymbeline*

Fear no more the heat o' the sun

Fear no more the heat o' the sun,
   Nor the furious winter's rages.
Thou thy worldly task hast done,
   Home art gone and ta'en thy wages.
Golden lads and girls all must,
As chimney sweepers, come to dust.

Fear no more the frown o' the great.
   Thou art past the tyrant's stroke.
Care no more to clothe and eat.
   To thee the reed is as the oak.
The scepter, learning, physic, must
All follow this and come to dust.

Fear no more the lightning flash,
   Nor the all-dreaded thunderstone.
Fear not slander, censure rash.
   Thou hast finished joy and moan.
All lovers young, all lovers must
Consign to thee and come to dust.

No exorciser harm thee!
Nor no witchcraft charm thee!
Ghost unlaid forbear thee!
Nothing ill come near thee!
Quiet consummation have,
And renowned be thy grave!

THOMAS NASHE   (c. 1567-1601)

from *Summer's Last Will and Testament*

Adieu, farewell

Adieu, farewell earth's bliss,
This world uncertain is;
Fond are life's lustful joys,
Death proves them all but toys,
None from his darts can fly.
I am sick, I must die.
      Lord, have mercy on us!

Rich men, trust not in wealth,
Gold cannot buy you health;
Physic himself must fade,
All things to end are made.
The plague full swift goes by.
I am sick, I must die.
      Lord, have mercy on us!

Beauty is but a flower
Which wrinkles will devour;
Brightness falls from the air,
Queens have died young and fair,
Dust hath closed Helen's eye.
I am sick, I must die.
      Lord, have mercy on us!

Strength stoops unto the grave,
Worms feed on Hector brave,
Swords may not fight with fate,
Earth still holds ope her gate.
Come! come! the bells do cry.
I am sick, I must die.
      Lord, have mercy on us!

Wit with his wantonness
Tasteth death's bitterness;
Hell's executioner
Hath no ears for to hear
What vain art can reply.
I am sick, I must die.
　　Lord, have mercy on us!

Haste, therefore, each degree
To welcome destiny.
Heaven is our heritage,
Earth but a player's stage;
Mount we unto the sky.
I am sick, I must die.
　　Lord, have mercy on us!

from *Summer's Last Will and Testament*

Autumn hath all

Autumn hath all the summer's fruitful treasure;
Gone is our sport, fled is poor Croydon's pleasure.
Short days, sharp days, long nights come on apace,
Ah! who shall hide us from the winter's face?
Cold doth increase, the sickness will not cease,
And here we lie, God knows, with little ease.
　　From winter, plague, and pestilence, good Lord, deliver us!

London doth mourn, Lambeth is quite forlorn;
Trades cry, woe worth that ever they were born.
The want of term is town and city's harm;
Close chambers we do want, to keep us warm.
Long banished must we live from our friends;
This low-built house will bring us to our ends.
　　From winter, plague, and pestilence, good Lord, deliver us!

THOMAS CAMPION (c. 1567-1619)

Now winter nights enlarge

Now winter nights enlarge
  The number of their hours,
And clouds their storms discharge
  Upon the airy towers.
Let now the chimneys blaze,
  And cups o'erflow with wine;
Let well-tuned words amaze
  With harmony divine.
Now yellow waxen lights
  Shall wait on honey Love,
While youthful revels, masks, and courtly sights
  Sleep's leaden spells remove.

This time doth well dispense
  With lovers' long discourse.
Much speech hath some defence
  Though beauty no remorse.
All do not all things well:
  Some measures comely tread,
Some knotted riddles tell,
  Some poems smoothly read.
The Summer hath his joys,
  And Winter his delights.
Though Love and all his pleasures are but toys,
  They shorten tedious nights.

To an Inconstant One

I loved thee once; I'll love no more—
    Thine be the grief as is the blame;
Thou art not what thou wast before,
    What reason I should be the same?
        He that can love unloved again,
        Hath better store of love than brain:
    God send me love my debts to pay,
    While unthrifts fool their love away!

Nothing could have my love o'erthrown
    If thou hadst still continued mine;
Yea, if thou hadst remained thy own,
    I might perchance have yet been thine.
        But thou thy freedom didst recall
        That it thou might elsewhere enthral:
    And then how could I but disdain
    A captive's captive to remain?

When new desires had conquered thee
    And changed the object of thy will,
It had been lethargy in me,
    Not constancy, to love thee still.
        Yea, it had been a sin to go
        And prostitute affection so:
    Since we are taught no prayers to say
    To such as must to others pray.

Yet do thou glory in thy choice—
    Thy choice of his good fortune boast;
I'll neither grieve nor yet rejoice
    To see him gain what I have lost:
        The height of my disdain shall be
        To laugh at him, to blush for thee;
    To love thee still, but go no more
    A-begging at a beggar's door.

BEN JONSON   (c. 1572-1637)

On My First Son

Farewell, thou child of my right hand, and joy;
My sin was too much hope of thee, loved boy,
Seven years tho'wert lent to me, and I thee pay,
Exacted by thy fate, on the just day.
O, could I loose all father, now. For why
Will man lament the state he should envy?
To have so soon 'scaped world's, and flesh's rage,
And, if no other misery, yet age?
Rest in soft peace, and, asked, say here doth lie
Ben. Jonson his best piece of poetry.
For whose sake, hence-forth, all his vows be such,
As what he loves my never like too much.

To the World

A Farewell for a Gentlewoman, Virtuous and Noble

False world, goodnight: since thou hast brought
   That hour upon my morn of age,
Henceforth I quit thee from my thought,
   My part is ended on thy stage.
Do not once hope, that thou canst tempt
   A spirit so resolved to tread
Upon thy throat, and live exempt
   From all the nets that thou canst spread.
I know thy forms are studied arts,
   Thy subtle ways, be narrow straits;
Thy courtesy by sudden starts,
   And what thou call'st thy gifts are baits.
I know too, though thou strut, and paint,
   Yet art thou both shrunk up, and old,.
That only fools make thee a saint,
   And all thy good is to be sold.
I know thou whole art but a shop
   Of toys, and trifles, traps, and snares,
To take the weak, or make them stop:
   Yet art thou falser then thy wares.
And, knowing this, should I yet stay,
   Like such as blow away their lives,
And never will redeem a day,
   Enamored of their golden gyves?
Or, having 'scaped, shall I return,
   And thrust my neck into the noose,
From whence, so lately, I did burn,
   With all my powers, my self to loose?
What bird, or beast, is known so dull,
   That fled his cage, or broke his chain,
And tasting air, and freedom, wull
   Render his head in there again?
If these, who have but sense, can shun
   The engines, that have them annoyed;
Little, for me, had reason done,
   If I could not thy ginnes avoid.
Yes, threaten, do. Alas I fear
   As little, as I hope from thee:
I know thou canst nor show, nor bear
   More hatred, then thou hast to me.
My tender, first, and simple years

Thou did'st abuse, and then betray;
Since stird'st up jealousies and fears,
    When all the causes were away.
Then, in a soil hast planted me,
    Where breathe the basest of thy fools;
Where envious arts professed be,
    And pride, and ignorance the schools,
Where nothing is examined, weighed,
    But, as 'tis rumored, so believed:
Where every freedom is betrayed,
    And every goodness taxed, or grieved.
But, what we're born for, we must bear:
    Our frail condition it is such,
That, what to all may happen here,
    If't chance to me, I must not grutch.
Else, I my state should much mistake,
    To harbour a divided thought
From all my kind: that, for my sake,
    There should a miracle be wrought.
No, I do know, that I was born
    To age, misfortune, sickness, grief:
But I will bear these, with that scorn,
    As shall not need thy false relief.
Nor for my peace will I go far,
    As wanderers do, that still do roam,
But make my strengths, such as they are,
    Here in my bosom, and at home.

To Heaven

Good and great God, can I not think of Thee,
But it must straight my melancholy be?
Is it interpreted in me disease,
That, laden with my sins, I seek for ease?
O, be Thou witness, that the reins dost know
And hearts of all, if I be sad for show;
And judge me after, if I dare pretend
To aught but grace, or aim at other end.
As Thou art all, so be Thou all to me,
First, midst, and last, converted One and Three;
My faith, my hope, my love; and in this state,
My judge, my witness, and my advocate.
Where have I been this while exiled from Thee?
And whither rap'd, now Thou but stoop'st to me?
Dwell, dwell here still! O, being everywhere,
How can I doubt to find Thee ever here?
I know my state, both full of shame and scorn,
Conceived in sin, and unto labor born,
Standing with fear, and must with horror fall,
And destined unto judgment, after all.
I feel my griefs too, and there scarce is ground
Upon my flesh t'inflict another wound.
Yet dare I not complain or wish for death
With holy Paul, lest it be thought the breath
Of discontent; or that these prayers be
For weariness of life, not love of Thee.

from *A Celebration of Charis*

1. His excuse for loving

Let it not your wonder move,
Less your laughter, that I love.
Though I now write fifty years,
I have had, and have my peers:
Poets, though divine, are men;
Some have loved as old again.
And it is not always face,
Clothes, or fortune gives the grace,
Or the feature, or the youth;
But the language and the truth,
With the ardor and the passion,
Gives the lover weight and fashion.
If you then will read the story,
First, prepare you to be sorry
That you never knew till now
Either whom to love, or how;
But be glad, as soon with me,
When you know that this is she
Of whose beauty it was sung,
She shall make the old man young,
Keep the middle age at stay,
And let nothing high decay,
Till she be the reason why
All the world for love may die.

2. How he saw her

I beheld her on a day
When her look out-flourished May,
And her dressing did out-brave
All the pride the fields then have;
Far I was from being stupid,
For I ran and called on Cupid:
"Love, if thou wilt ever see
Mark of glory, come with me;
Where's thy quiver? Bend thy bow;
Here's a shaft; thou art too slow!"
And, withal, I did untie
Every cloud about his eye;
But he had not gained his sight
Sooner than he lost his might
Or his courage; for away
Straight he ran, and durst not stay,
Letting bow and arrow fall;
Nor for any threat or call
Could be brought once back to look.
I, fool-hardy, there uptook
Both the arrow he had quit
And the bow, which thought to hit
This my object. But she threw
Such a lightning as I drew
At my face, that took my sight
And my motion from me quite;
So that, there, I stood a stone,
Mocked of all; and called of one
(Which with grief and wrath I heard)
Cupid's statue with a beard,
Or else one that played his ape,
In a Hercules—his shape.

My Picture Left in Scotland

I now think Love is rather deaf than blind,
    For else it could not be
      That she
Whom I adore so much should so slight me,
    And cast my love behind.
I'm sure my language to her was as sweet,
    And every close did meet
   In sentence of as subtle feet
    As hath the youngest he
That sits in shadow of Apollo's tree.

   Oh, but my conscious fears
     That fly my thoughts between,
     Tell me that she hath seen
    My hundreds of gray hairs,
    Told seven and forty years,
  Read so much waste, as she cannot embrace
  My mountain belly and my rocky face;
And all these through her eyes have stopped her ears.

An Elegy

Though beauty be the mark of praise,
   And yours of whom I sing be such
   As not the world can praise too much,
Yet is't your virtue now I raise.

A virtue, like allay, so gone
   Throughout your form, as though that move,
   And draw, and conquer all men's love,
This subjects you to love of one,

Wherein you triumph yet: because
   'Tis of your self, and that you use
   The noblest freedom, not to choose
Against or faith, or honor's laws.

But who should less expect from you,
   In whom alone love lives again?
   By whom he is restored to men,
And kept, and bred, and brought up true.

His falling temples you have reared,
   The withered garlands ta'en away,
   His altars kept from the decay
That envy wished and nature feared;

And on them burn so chaste a flame
   With so much loyalty's expense,
   As Love, to acquit such excellence,
Is gone himself into your name.

And you are he: the deity
   To whom all lovers are designed,
   That would their better objects find—
Among which faithful troop am I,

Who as an offering at your shrine
   Have sung this hymn, and here entreat
   One spark of your diviner heat
To light upon a love of mine,

Which, if it kindle not, but scant
   Appear, and that to shortest view,
   Yet give me leave t'adore in you
What I, in her, am grieved to want.

from *Cynthia's Revels*

Hymn to Diana

Queen and huntress, chaste and fair,
  Now the sun is laid to sleep,
Seated in thy silver chair
  State in wonted manner keep:
Hesperus entreats thy light,
Goddess excellently bright.

Earth, let not thy envious shade
  Dare itself to interpose;
Cynthia's shining orb was made
  Heaven to clear, when day did close;
Bless us then with wished sight,
Goddess excellently bright.

Lay thy bow of pearl apart,
  And thy crystal shining quiver;
Give unto the flying hart
  Space to breathe, how short soever,
Thou that mak'st a day of night,
Goddess excellently bright.

An Ode to Himself

Where dost thou careless lie
   Buried in ease and sloth?
Knowledge, that sleeps, doth die;
And this security,
   It is the common moth,
That eats on wits, and arts, and oft destroys them both.

Are all the Aonian springs
   Dried up? lies Thespia waste?
Doth Clarius' harp want strings,
That not a nymph now sings!
   Or droop they as disgraced,
To see their seats and bowers by chattering pies defaced?

If hence thy silence be,
   As 'tis too just a cause;
Let this thought quicken thee,
Minds that are great and free,
   Should not on fortune pause,
'Tis crown enough to virtue still, her own applause.

What though the greedy fry
   Be taken with false baits
Of worded Balladry,
And think it poesy?
   They die with their conceits,
And only pitous scorn, upon their folly waits.

Then take in hand thy lyre,
   Strike in thy proper strain,
With Japhet's line, aspire
Sol's chariot for new fire,
   To give the world again:
Who aided him will thee, the issue of Jove's brain.

And since our dainty age
   Cannot endure reproof,
Make not thyself a page,
To that strumpet the stage
   But sing high and aloof,
Safe from the wolves' black jaw, and the dull ass's hoof.

JOHN DONNE   (c. 1572-1631)

from *Holy Sonnets*

VII

At the round earth's imagined corners, blow
Your trumpets, angels, and arise, arise
From death, you numberless infinities
Of souls, and to your scattered bodies go,
All whom the flood did, and fire shall o'erthrow,
All whom war, dearth, age, agues, tyrannies,
Despair, law, chance hath slain, and you whose eyes
Shall behold God and never taste death's woe.
But let them sleep, Lord, and me mourn a space,
For if above all these my sins abound,
'Tis late to ask abundance of thy grace
When we are there. Here on this lowly ground
Teach me how to repent, for that's as good
As if thou'dst sealed my pardon with thy blood.

A Valediction: Of My Name In The Window

I

My name engraved herein
Doth contribute my firmness to this glass,
Which, ever since that charm, hath been
As hard as that which graved it was;
Thine eye will give it price enough to mock
The diamonds of either rock.

II

'Tis much that glass should be
As all-confessing and through-shine as I;
'Tis more, that it shows thee to thee
And clear reflects thee to thine eye.
But all such rules, love's magic can undo;
Here you see me, and I am you.

III

As no one point nor dash,
Which are but accessaries to this name,
The showers and tempests can outwash,
So shall all times find me the same;
You this entireness better may fulfil,
Who have the pattern with you still.

IV

Or if too hard and deep
This learning be for a scratched name to teach,
It as a given death's head keep
Lovers' mortality to preach,
Or think this ragged bony name to be
My ruinous anatomy.

V

Then, as all my souls be
Emparadised in you (in whom alone
I understand and grow and see),
The rafters of my body, bone
Being still with you, the muscle, sinew, and vein
Which tile this house will come again.

VI

Till my return, repair
And recompact my scattered body so.
As all the virtuous powers which are
Fixed in the stars are said to flow
Into such characters as graved be
When these stars have supremacy.

VII

So, since this name was cut
When love and grief their exaltation had,
No door 'gainst this name's influence shut.
As much more loving as more sad
'Twill make thee; and thou shouldst, till I return,
Since I die daily, daily mourn.

VIII

When thy inconsiderate hand
Flings ope this casement with my trembling name
To look on one whose wit or land
New battery to thy heart may frame,
Then think this name alive, and that thou thus
In it offendst my Genius.

IX

And when thy melted maid,
Corrupted by thy lover's gold and page,
His letter at thy pillow hath laid,
Disputed it, and tamed thy rage,
And thou beginst to thaw towards him, for this,
May my name step in and hide his.

X

And if this treason go
To an overt act, and that thou write again,
In superscribing, this name flow
Into thy fancy from the pane.
So, in forgetting thou remembrest right,
And unaware to me shall write.

XI

But glass and lines must be
No means our firm substantial love to keep;
Near death inflicts this lethargy,
And this I murmur in my sleep:
Impute this idle talk to that I go,
For dying men talk often so.

JOHN WEBSTER   (c. 1580-c. 1630)

from *The Duchess of Malfi*

Hark! Now everything is still

Hark! Now everything is still,
The screech-owl and the whistler shrill,
Call upon our dame aloud,
And bid her quickly don her shroud!
Much you had of land and rent;
Your length in clay's now competent:
A long war disturbed your mind;
Here your perfect peace is signed.
Of what is't fools make such vain keeping?
Sin their conception, their birth weeping,
Their life a general mist of error,
Their death a hideous storm of terror.
Strew your hair with powders sweet,
Don clean linen, bathe your feet,
And—the foul fiend more to check—
A crucifix let bless your neck:
'Tis now full tide 'tween night and day;
End your groan and come away.

LORD HERBERT OF CHERBURY   (1583-1648)

Elegy Over a Tomb

Must I then see, alas! eternal night
    Sitting upon those fairest eyes,
And closing all those beams, which once did rise
    So radiant and bright,
That light and heat in them to us did prove
    Knowledge and Love?

Oh, if you did delight no more to stay
    Upon this low and earthly stage,
But rather chose an endless heritage,
    Tell us at least, we pray,
Where all the beauties that those ashes owed
    Are now bestowed?

Doth the sun now his light with yours renew?
    Have waves the curling of your hair?
Did you restore unto the sky and air,
    The red, and white, and blue?
Have you vouchsafed to flowers since your death
    That sweetest breath?

Had not heaven's lights else in their houses slept,
    Or to some private life retired?
Must not the sky and air have else conspired?
    And in their regions wept?
Must not each flower else the earth could breed
    Have been a weed?

But thus enriched may we not yield some cause
    Why they themselves lament no more?
That must have changed the course they held before,
    And broke their proper laws,
Had not your beauties given this second birth
    To heaven and earth?

Tell us—for oracles must still ascend,
    For those that crave them at your tomb—
Tell us, where are those beauties now become,
    And what they now intend:
Tell us, alas, that cannot tell our grief,
    Or hope relief.

HENRY KING   (1592-1669)

The Exequy

Accept thou Shrine of my dead Saint,
Instead of Dirges this complaint;
And for sweet flowers to crown thy hearse,
Receive a strew of weeping verse
From thy grieved friend, whom thou might'st see
Quite melted into tears for thee.

Dear loss! since thy untimely fate
My task hath been to meditate
On thee, on thee: thou art the book,
The library whereon I look
Though almost blind. For thee (loved clay)
I languish out not live the day,
Using no other exercise
But what I practice with mine eyes:
By which wet glasses I find out
How lazily time creeps about
To one that mourns: this, only this
My exercise and business is:
So I compute the weary hours
With sighs dissolved into showers.

Nor wonder if my time go thus
Backward and most preposterous;
Thou hast benighted me, thy set
This Eve of blackness did beget,
Who wast my day, (though overcast
Before thou had'st thy Noon-tide past)
And I remember must in tears,
Thou scarce had'st seen so many years
As Day tells hours. By thy clear Sun
My love and fortune first did run;
But thou wilt never more appear
Folded within my Hemisphere,
Since both thy light and motion
Like a fled Star is fallen and gone,
And twixt me and my soul's dear wish
The earth now interposed is,
Which such a strange eclipse doth make
As ne'er was read in Almanake.

I could allow thee for a time
To darken me and my sad Clime,
Were it a month, a year, or ten,
I would thy exile live till then;
And all that space my mirth adjourn,
So thou wouldst promise to return;
And putting off thy ashy shroud
At length disperse this sorrow's cloud.

But woe is me! the longest date
Too narrow is to calculate
These empty hopes: never shall I
Be so much blessed as to descry
A glimpse of thee, till that day come
Which shall the earth to cinders doom,
And a fierce fever must calcine
The body of this world like thine,
(My Little World!); that fit of fire
Once off, our bodies shall aspire
To our soul's bliss: then we shall rise,
And view ourselves with clearer eyes
In that calm Region, where no night
Can hide us from each other's sight.

Mean time, thou hast her, earth: much good
May my harm do thee. Since it stood
With Heaven's will I might not call
Her longer mine, I give thee all
My short-lived right and interest
In her, whom living I loved best:
With a most free and bounteous grief,
I give thee what I could not keep.
Be kind to her, and prithee look
Thou write into thy Doom's-day book
Each parcel of this Rarity
Which in thy Casket shrined doth lie:
See that thou make thy reckoning straight,
And yield her back again by weight;
For thou must audit on thy trust
Each grain and atom of this dust,
As thou wilt answer *Him* that lent,
Not gave thee, my dear Monument.

So close the ground, and 'bout her shade
Black curtains draw, my *Bride* is laid.

Sleep on my *Love* in thy cold bed
Never to be disquieted!
My last good night! Thou wilt not wake
Till I thy fate shall overtake:
Till age, or grief, or sickness must
Marry my body to that dust
It so much loves; and fill the room
My heart keeps empty in thy Tomb.
Stay for me there; I will not fail
To meet thee in that hallow Vale.
And think not much of my delay;
I am already on the way,
And follow thee with all the speed
Desire can make, or sorrows breed.
Each minute is a short degree,
And every hour a step towards thee.
At night when I betake to rest,
Next morn I rise nearer my West
Of life, almost by eight hour's sail,
Than when sleep breathed his drowsy gale.

Thus from the Sun my Bottom steers,
And my days Compass downward bears:
Nor labor I to stem the tide
Through which to *Thee* I swiftly glide.

'Tis true, with shame and grief I yield,
Thou like the *Van* first took'st the field,
And gotten hast the victory
In thus adventuring to die
Before me, whose more years might crave
A just precedence in the grave.
But heark! My Pulse like a soft Drum
Beats my approach, tells *Thee* I come;
And slow howe'er my marches be,
I shall at last sit down by *Thee*.

The thought of this bids me go on,
And wait my dissolution
With hope and comfort. *Dear* (forgive
The crime) I am content to live
Divided, with but half a heart,
Till we shall meet and never part.

GEORGE HERBERT   (1593-1633)

Church Monuments

While that my soul repairs to her devotion,
Here I intomb my flesh, that it betimes
May take acquaintance of this heap of dust;
To which the blast of death's incessant motion,
Fed with the exhalation of our crimes,
Drives all at last. Therefore I gladly trust

My body to this school, that it may learn
To spell his elements, and find his birth
Written in dusty heraldry and lines;
Which dissolution sure doth best discern,
Comparing dust with dust, and earth with earth.
These laugh at jet, and marble put for signs,

To sever the good fellowship of dust,
And spoil the meeting. What shall point out them,
When they shall bow, and kneel, and fall down flat
To kiss those heaps, which now they have in trust?
Dear flesh, while I do pray, learn here thy stem
And true descent; that when thou shalt grow fat,

And wanton in thy cravings, thou mayst know,
That flesh is but the glass, which holds the dust
That measures all our time; which also shall
Be crumbled into dust. Mark, here below,
How tame these ashes are, how free from lust,
That thou mayst fit thyself against thy fall.

ROBERT HERRICK   (1591-1674)

To the Virgins, to make much of Time

Gather ye rosebuds while ye may,
  Old Time is still a flying:
And this same flower that smiles today,
  Tomorrow will be dying.

The glorious lamp of heaven, the sun,
  The higher he's a getting;
The sooner will his race be run,
  And nearer he's to setting.

That age is best, which is the first,
  When youth and blood are warmer;
But being spent, the worse, and worst
  Times still succeed the former.

Then be not coy, but use your time;
  And while ye may, go marry:
For having lost but once your prime,
  You may forever tarry.

His Poetry his Pillar

Only a little more
  I have to write,
  Then I'll give o'er,
And bid the world goodnight.

'Tis but a flying minute,
  That I must stay,
  Or linger in it;
And then I must away.

O time that cut'st down all!
  And scarce leav'st here
  Memorial
Of any men that were.

How many lie forgot
  In vaults beneath?
  And piece-meal rot
Without a fame in death?

Behold this living stone,
   I rear for me,
   Ne'er to be thrown
Down, envious Time, by thee.

Pillars let some set up,
   (If so they please)
   Here is my hope,
And my *Pyramides*.

To Music, to becalm his Fever

Charm me asleep, and melt me so
   With thy delicious numbers;
That being ravished, hence I go
   Away in easy slumbers.
      Ease my sick head,
      And make my bed,
Thou Power that canst sever
      From me this ill:
      And quickly still:
      Though thou not kill
         My fever.

Thou sweetly canst convert the same
   From a consuming fire,
Into a gentle-licking flame,
   And make it thus expire.
      Then make me weep
      My pains asleep;
And give me such reposes,
      That I, poor I,
      May think, thereby,
      I live and die
         'Mongst roses.

Fall on me like a silent dew,
   Or like those maiden showers,
Which, by the peep of day, do strew
   A baptime o'er the flowers.
      Melt, melt my pains,
      With thy soft strains;
That having ease me given,
      With full delight,
      I leave this light;
      And take my flight
         For Heaven.

To Meadows

Ye have been fresh and green,
  Ye have been filled with flowers:
And ye the walks have been
  Where maids have spent their hours.

You have beheld, how they
  With *Wicker Arks* did come
To kiss, and bear away
  The richer cowslips home.

Y'ave heard them sweetly sing,
  And seen them in a round:
Each virgln, like a spring,
  With honeysuckles crowned.

But now, we see, none here,
  Whose silvery feet did tread,
And with dishevelled hair,
  Adorned this smoother mead.

Like unthrifts, having spent,
  Your stock, and needy grown,
Y'are left here to lament
  Your poor estates, alone.

To the Yew and Cypress to grace his Funeral

      Both you two have
    Relation to the grave:
            And where
The *Fun'ral-Trump* sounds, you are there.

        I shall be made
    Ere long a fleeting shade:
          Pray come,
And do some honor to my tomb.

        Do not deny
    My last request; for I
            Will be
Thankful to you, or friends, for me.

To Daffodils

Fair daffodils, we weep to see
   You haste away so soon:
As yet the early-rising sun
   Has not attained his noon.
      Stay, stay,
    Until the hasting day
        Has run
    But to the evensong;
And, having prayed together, we
     Will go with you along.

We have short time to stay, as you,
   We have as short a spring;
As quick a growth to meet decay,
   As you, or any thing.
      We die,
    As your hours do, and dry
       Away,
   Like to the summer's rain;
Or as the pearls of morning's dew
    Ne'er to be found again.

Upon his departure hence

Thus I
Pass by,
And die:
As One,
Unknown,
And gone:
I'm made
A shade,
And laid
I'th' grave:
There have
My cave,
Where tell
I dwell.
Farewell.

His Litany, to the Holy Spirit

In the hour of my distress,
When temptations me oppress,
And when I my sins confess,
    Sweet Spirit, comfort me!

When I lie within my bed,
Sick in Heart, and sick in head,
And with doubts discomforted,
    Sweet Spirit, comfort me!

When the house doth sigh and weep,
And the world is drowned in sleep,
Yet mine eyes the watch do keep;
    Sweet Spirit, comfort me!

When the artless doctor sees
No one hope, but of his fees,
And his skill runs on the lees;
    Sweet Spirit, comfort me!

When his potion and his pill,
Has, or none, or little skill,
Meet for nothing, but to kill;
    Sweet Spirit, comfort me!

When the passing-bell doth toll,
And the Furies in a shoal
Come to fright a parting soul;
    Sweet Spirit, comfort me!

When the tapers now burn blue,
And the comforters are few,
And that number more than true;
    Sweet Spirit, comfort me!

When the Priest his last hath prayed,
And I nod to what is said,
'Cause my speech is now decayed;
    Sweet Spirit, comfort me!

When (God knows) I'm tossed about,
Either with despair, or doubt;
Yet before the glass be out,
    Sweet Spirit, comfort me!

When the Tempter me pursu'th
With the sins of all my youth,
And half damns me with untruth;
    Sweet Spirit, comfort me!

When the flames and hellish cries
Fright mine ears, and fright mine eyes,
And all terrors me surprise;
    Sweet Spirit, comfort me!

When the Judgment is revealed,
And that opened which was sealed,
When to Thee I have appealed;
    Sweet Spirit, comfort me!

Epitaph on the Tomb of Sir Edward Giles and His Wife
in the South Aisle of Dean Prior Church, Devon

No trust to metals nor to marbles, when
These have their fate and wear away as men;
Times, titles, trophies may be lost and spent,
But virtue rears the eternal monument.
What more than these can tombs or tombstones pay?
But here's the sunset of a tedious day:
These two asleep are: I'll but be undressed
And so to bed: pray wish us all good rest.

ANDREW MARVELL   (1621-1678)

The Garden

How vainly men themselves amaze
To win the palm, the oak, or bays,
And their uncessant labors see
Crowned from some single herb or tree,
Whose short and narrow-verged shade
Does prudently their toils upbraid;
While all the flowers and trees do close
To weave the garlands of repose!

Fair Quiet, have I found thee here,
And Innocence thy sister dear?
Mistaken long, I sought you then
In busy companies of men:
Your sacred plants, if here below,
Only among the plants will grow:
Society is all but rude
To this delicious solitude.

No white nor red was ever seen
So amorous as this lovely green.
Fond lovers, cruel as their flame,
Cut in these trees their mistress' name:
Little, alas! they know or heed
How far these beauties hers exceed!
Fair trees! wheres'e'er your barks I wound,
No name shall but your own be found.

When we have run our passions' heat,
Love hither makes his best retreat:
The gods, that mortal beauty chase,
Still in a tree did end their race;
Apollo hunted Daphne so
Only that she might laurel grow;
And Pan did after Syrinx speed
Not as a nymph, but for a reed.

What wondrous life in this I lead!
Ripe apples drop about my head;
The luscious clusters of the vine
Upon my mouth do crush their wine;
The nectarine and curious peach
Into my hands themselves do reach;
Stumbling on melons, as I pass,
Ensnared with flowers, I fall on grass.

Meanwhile the mind from pleasure less
Withdraws into its happiness;
The mind, that Ocean where each kind
Does straight its own resemblance find;
Yet it creates, transcending these,
Far other worlds, and other seas;
Annihilating all that's made
To a green thought in a green shade.

Here at the fountain's sliding foot,
Or at some fruit-tree's mossy root,
Casting the body's vest aside,
My soul into the boughs does glide;
There, like a bird, it sits and sings,
Then whets and combs its silver wings,
And, till prepared for longer flight,
Waves in its plumes the various light.

Such was that happy Garden-state
While man there walked without a mate:
After a place so pure and sweet,
What other help could yet be meet!
But 'twas beyond a mortal's share
To wander solitary there:
Two paradises 'twere in one,
To live in Paradise alone.

How well the skillful gardener drew
Of flowers and herbs this dial new!
Where, from above, the milder sun
Does through a fragrant zodiac run:
And, as it works, the industrious bee
Computes its time as well as we.
How could such sweet and wholesome hours
Be reckoned, but with herbs and flowers!

PHILIP PAIN   (?-c. 1666)
American?

   Meditation 8

   Scarce do I pass a day, but that I hear
   Some one or other's dead, and to my ear
   Me thinks it is no news. But oh! did I
   Think deeply on it, what it is to die,
      My pulses all would beat, I should not be
      Drowned in this deluge of security.

HENRY VAUGHAN   (1622-1695)

   To His Books

   Bright books! the perspectives to our weak sights,
   The clear projections of discerning lights,
   Burning and shining thoughts, man's posthume day,
   The track of fled souls, and their milky-way,
   The dead alive and busy, the still voice
   Of enlarged spirits, kind heaven's white decoys!
   Who lives with you, lives like those knowing flowers,
   Which in commerce with light spend all their hours;
   Which shut to clouds, and shadows nicely shun,
   But with glad haste unveil to kiss the sun.
   Beneath you all is dark and a dead night,
   Which whoso lives in, wants both health and sight.
      By sucking you, the wise (like bees) do grow
   Healing and rich, though this they do most slow,
   Because most choicely, for as great a store
   Have we of books, as bees of herbs, or more:
   And the great task to try, then know, the good,
   To discern weeds, and judge of wholesome food,
   Is a rare, scant performance; for man dies
   Oft ere 'tis done, while the bee feeds and flies.
   But you were all choice flowers, all set and dressed
   By old, sage florists, who well knew the best:
   And I amidst you all am turned a weed!
   Not wanting knowledge, but for want of heed.
   Then thank thyself, wild fool, that would'st not be
   Content to know—what was too much for thee!

The Lamp

'Tis dead night round about: Horror doth creep
And move on with the shades; stars nod and sleep,
And through the dark air spin a fiery thread,
Such as doth gild the lazy glow-worm's bed.
   Yet burn'st thou here a full day, while I spend
My rest in cares, and to the dark world lend
These flames, as thou dost thine to me; I watch
That hour, which must thy life and mine dispatch,
But still thou dost out-go me. I can see
Met in thy flames all acts of piety;
Thy light is Charity, thy heat is Zeal,
And thy aspiring, active fires reveal
Devotion still on wing; Then, thou dost weep
Still as thou burn'st, and the warm droppings creep
To measure out thy length, as if thou'dst know
What stock, and how much time were left thee now.
Nor dost thou spend one tear in vain, for still
As thou dissolv'st to them, and they distill,
They're stored up in the socket, where they lie,
When all is spent, thy last and sure supply.
And such is true repentance; every breath
We spend in sighs is treasure after death.
Only, one point escapes thee: That thy oil
Is still out with thy flame, and so both fail.
But whensoe're I'm out, both shall be in,
And where thou mad'st an end, there I'll begin.

Mark Cap. 13, ver. 35.
   *Watch you therefore, for you know not when the master of
the house commeth, at Even, or at midnight, or at the Cock-
crowing, or in the morning.*

THOMAS TRAHERNE   (1637-1674)

On News

News from a foreign country came
As if my treasure and my wealth lay there;
So much it did my heart inflame,
'Twas wont to call my soul into mine ear;
    Which thither went to meet
    The approaching sweet,
   And on the threshold stood
To entertain the unknown good.
    It hovered there
   As if 'twould leave mine ear,
And was so eager to embrace
  The joyful tidings as they came,
'Twould almost leave its dwelling-place
   To entertain that same.

As if the tidings were the things,
My very joys themselves, my foreign treasure—
Or else did bear them on their wings—
With so much joy they came, with so much pleasure.
    My soul stood at that gate
    To recreate
   Itself with bliss, and to
Be pleased with speed. A fuller view
    It fain would take
   Yet journeys back would make
Unto my heart; as if 'twould fain
  Go out to meet, yet stay within
To fit a place to entertain
   And bring the tidings in.

What sacred instinct did inspire
My soul in childhood with a hope so strong?
What secret force moved my desire
To expect my joys beyond the seas, so young?
    Felicity I knew
      Was out of view,
   And being here alone,
I saw that happiness was gone
    From me! For this
    I thirsted absent bliss,
And thought that sure beyond the seas,
  Or else in something near at hand—
I knew not yet—since naught did please
  I knew—my bliss did stand.

But little did the infant dream
That all the treasures of the world were by:
  And that himself was so the cream
And crown of all which round about did lie.
    Yet thus it was: the gem,
      The diadem,
    The ring enclosing all
That stood upon this earthly ball,
    The heavenly eye,
   Much wider than the sky,
Wherein they all included were,
  The glorious soul, that was the king
Made to possess them, did appear
    A small and little thing!

JOHN DRYDEN (1631-1700)

MacFlecknoe

Or, A Satire Upon the True-Blue-Protestant Poet T.S.

All human things are subject to decay,
And when fate summons, monarchs must obey.
This Flecknoe found, who, like Augustus, young
Was called to empire, and had governed long;
In prose and verse, was owned, without dispute,
Through all the realms of *Nonsense*, absolute.
This aged prince, now flourishing in peace,
And blest with issue of a large increase;
Worn out with business, did at length debate
To settle the succession of the State;
And, pondering which of all his sons was fit
To reign, and wage immortal war with wit,
Cried: " 'T is resolved; for nature pleads, that he
Should only rule, who most resembles me.
Sh—— alone my perfect image bears,
Mature in dullness from his tender years:
Sh—— alone, of all my sons, is he
Who stands confirmed in full stupidity.
The rest to some faint meaning make pretense,
But Sh—— never deviates into sense.
Some beams of wit on other souls may fall,
Strike through, and make a lucid interval;
But Sh——'s genuine night admits no ray,
His rising fogs prevail upon the day.
Besides, his goodly fabric fills the eye,
And seems designed for thoughtless majesty;
Thoughtless as monarch oaks that shade the plain,
And, spread in solemn state, supinely reign.
Heywood and Shirley were but types of thee,
Thou last great prophet of tautology.
Even I, a dunce of more renown than they,
Was sent before but to prepare thy way;
And, coarsely clad in Norwich drugget, came
To teach the nations in thy greater name.
My warbling lute, the lute I whilom strung,
When to King John of Portugal I sung,

Was but the prelude to that glorious day,
When thou on silver Thames didst cut thy way,
With well-timed oars before the royal barge,
Swelled with the pride of thy celestial charge;
And big with hymn, commander of a host,
The like was ne'er in Epsom blankets tossed.
Methinks I see the new Arion sail,
The lute still trembling underneath thy nail.
At thy well-sharpened thumb from shore to shore
The treble squeaks for fear, the basses roar;
Echoes from Pissing Alley Sh____ call,
And Sh____ they resound from Aston Hall.
About thy boat the little fishes throng,
As at the morning toast that floats along.
Sometimes, as prince of thy harmonious band,
Thou wield'st thy papers in thy threshing hand.
St. André's feet ne'er kept more equal time,
Not even the feet of thy own *Psyche's* rhyme;
Though they in number as in sense excel:
So just, so like tautology, they fell,
That, pale with envy, Singleton forswore
The lute and sword, which he in triumph bore,
And vowed he ne'er would act Villerius more."
Here stopped the good old sire, and wept for joy
In silent raptures of the hopeful boy.
All arguments, but most his plays, persuade,
That for anointed dullness he was made.
   Close to the walls which fair Augusta bind,
(The fair Augusta much to fears inclined,)
An ancient fabric raised t' inform the sight,
There stood of yore, and Barbican it hight:
A watchtower once; but now, so fate ordains,
Of all the pile an empty name remains.
From its old ruins brothel-houses rise,
Scenes of lewd loves, and of polluted joys,
Where their vast courts the mother-strumpets keep,
And, undisturbed by watch, in silence sleep.
Near these a Nursery erects its head,
Where queens are formed, and future heroes bred;
Where unfledged actors learn to laugh and cry,
Where infant punks their tender voices try,
And little Maximins the gods defy.
Great Fletcher never treads in buskins here,
Nor greater Jonson dares in socks appear;

But gentle Simkin just reception finds
Amidst this monument of vanished minds:
Pure clinches the suburbian Muse affords,
And Panton waging harmless war with words.
Here Flecknoe, as a place to fame well known,
Ambitiously designed his Sh——'s throne;
For ancient Dekker prophesied long since,
That in this pile should reign a mighty prince,
Born for a scourge of wit, and flail of sense;
To whom true dullness should some *Psyches* owe,
But worlds of *Misers* from his pen should flow;
Humorists and *Hypocrites* it should produce,
Whole Raymond families, and tribes of Bruce.
  Now Empress Fame had published the renown
Of Sh——'s coronation through the town.
Roused by report of Fame, the nations meet,
From near Bunhill, and distant Watling Street.
No Persian carpets spread the imperial way,
But scattered limbs of mangled poets lay;
From dusty shops neglected authors come,
Martyrs of pies, and relics of the bum.
Much Heywood, Shirley, Ogleby there lay,
But loads of Sh—— almost choked the way.
Bilked stationers for yeomen stood prepared,
And Herringman was captain of the guard.
The hoary prince in majesty appeared,
High on a throne of his own labors reared.
At his right hand our young Ascanius sate,
Rome's other hope, and pillar of the State.
His brows thick fogs, instead of glories, grace,
And lambent dullness played around his face.
As Hannibal did to the altars come,
Sworn by his sire a mortal foe to Rome;
So Sh—— swore, nor should his vow be vain,
That he till death true dullness would maintain;
And, in his father's right, and realm's defense,
Ne'er to have peace with wit, nor truce with sense.
The king himself the sacred unction made,
As king by office, and as priest by trade.
In his sinister hand, instead of ball,
He placed a mighty mug of potent ale;
Love's Kingdom to his right he did convey,
At once his scepter, and his rule of sway;
Whose righteous lore the prince had practiced young,

And from whose loins recorded *Psyche* sprung.
His temples, last, with poppies were o'erspread,
That nodding seemed to consecrate his head.
Just at that point of time, if fame not lie,
On his left hand twelve reverend owls did fly.
So Romulus, 't is sung, by Tiber's brook,
Presage of sway from twice six vultures took.
Th'admiring throng loud acclamations make,
And omens of his future empire take
The sire then shook the honors of his head,
And from his brows damps of oblivion shed
Full on the filial dullness: long he stood,
Repelling from his breast the raging god;
At length burst out in this prophetic mood:
   "Heavens bless my son, from Ireland let him reign
To far Barbadoes on the western main;
Of his dominion may no end be known,
And greater than his father's be his throne;
Beyond *Love's Kingdom* let him stretch his pen!"
He paused, and all the people cried, "Amen."
Then thus continued he: "My son, advance
Still in new impudence, new ignorance.
Success let others teach, learn thou from me
Pangs without birth, and fruitless industry.
Let *Virtuosos* in five years be writ;
Yet not one thought accuse thy toil of wit.
Let gentle George in triumph tread the stage,
Make Dorimant betray, and Loveit rage;
Let Cully, Cockwood, Fopling, charm the pit,
And in their folly shew the writer's wit.
Yet still thy fools shall stand in thy defense,
And justify their author's want of sense.
Let 'em be all by thy own model made
Of dullness, and desire no foreign aid;
That they to future ages may be known,
Not copies drawn, but issue of thy own.
Nay, let thy men of wit too be the same,
All full of thee, and differing but in name,
But let no alien S—dl—y interpose,
To lard with wit thy hungry *Epsom* prose.
And when false flowers of rhetoric thou wouldst cull,
Trust nature, do not labor to be dull;
But write thy best, and top; and, in each line,
Sir Formal's oratory will be thine:

Sir Formal, though unsought, attends thy quill,
And does thy northern dedications fill.
Nor let false friends seduce thy mind to fame,
By arrogating Jonson's hostile name.
Let father Flecknoe fire thy mind with praise,
And uncle Ogleby thy envy raise.
Thou art my blood, where Jonson has no part:
What share have we in nature, or in art?
Where did his wit on learning fix a brand,
And rail at arts he did not understand?
Where made he love in Prince Nicander's vein,
Or swept the dust in *Psyche's* humble strain?
Where sold he bargains, 'whip-stitch, kiss my arse,
Promised a play and dwindled to a farce?
When did his Muse from Fletcher scenes purloin,
As thou whole Eth'rege dost transfuse to thine?
But so transfused, as oil on water's flow,
His always floats above, thine sinks below.
This is thy province, this thy wondrous way
New humors to invent for each new play:
This is that boasted bias of thy mind,
By which one way, to dullness, 't is inclined;
Which makes thy writings lean on one side still,
And, in all changes, that way bends thy will.
Nor let thy mountain-belly make pretense
Of likeness; thine's a tympany of sense.
A tun of man in thy large bulk is writ,
But sure thou'rt but a kilderkin of wit.
Like mine, thy gentle numbers feebly creep;
Thy tragic Muse gives smiles, thy comic sleep.
With whate'er gall thou sett'st thyself to write,
Thy inoffensive satires never bite.
In thy felonious heart though venom lies,
It does but touch thy Irish pen, and dies.
Thy genius calls thee not to purchase fame
In keen iambics, but mild anagram.
Leave writing plays, and choose for thy command
Some peaceful province in acrostic land.
There thou may'st wings display and altars raise,
And torture one poor word ten thousand ways.
Or, if thou wouldst thy different talents suit,
Set thy own songs, and sing them to thy lute."
   He said: but his last words were scarcely heard;
For Bruce and Longvil had a trap prepared,

And down they sent the yet declaiming bard.
Sinking he left his drugget robe behind,
Borne upwards by a subterranean wind.
The mantle fell to the young prophet's part,
With double portion of his father's art.

from *Secret Love, or the Maiden-Queen*

I feed a flame within

I feed a flame within, which so torments me
That it both pains my heart, and yet contents me:
'Tis such a pleasing smart, and I so love it,
That I had rather die than once remove it.

Yet he, for whom I grieve, shall never know it;
My tongue does not betray, nor my eyes show it.
Not a sigh, nor a tear, my pain discloses,
But they fall silently, like dew on roses.

Thus, to prevent my Love from being cruel,
My heart's the sacrifice, as 'tis the fuel;
And while I suffer this to give him quiet,
My faith rewards my love, though he deny it.

On his eyes will I gaze, and there delight me;
While I conceal my love no frown can fright me.
To be more happy I dare not aspire,
Nor can I fall more low, mounting no higher.

from *Cleomenes*

No, no, poor suffering heart

No, no, poor suffering heart, no change endeavor,
Choose to sustain the smart, rather than leave her;
My ravished eyes behold such charms about her,
I can die with her, but not live without her:
One tender sigh of hers to see me languish,
Will more than pay the price of my past anguish:
Beware, O cruel Fair, how you smile on me,
'Twas a kind look of yours that has undone me.

Love has in store for me one happy minute,
And she will end my pain who did begin it;
Then no day void of bliss, or pleasure leaving,
Ages shall slide away without perceiving:
Cupid shall guard the door the more to please us,
And keep out Time and Death, when thy would seize us:
Time and Death shall depart, and say in flying,
Love has found out a way to live, by dying.

CHARLES CHURCHILL   (1731-1764)

The Dedication to the Sermons

HEALTH to great GLOSTER—from a man unknown,
Who holds thy health as dearly as his own,
Accept this greeting—nor let modest fear
Call up one maiden blush—I mean not here
To wound with flattery—'tis a Villain's art,
And suits not with the frankness of my heart.
Truth best becomes an *Orthodox* Divine,
And, spite of hell, that Character is mine;
To speak e'en bitter truths I cannot fear;
But truth, *my Lord*, is panegyric here.

   Health to great GLOSTER—nor, through love of ease,
Which all Priests love, let this address displease.
I ask no favor, not one note I crave,
And, when this busy brain rests in the grave,
(For till that time it never can have rest)
I will not trouble you with one bequest.
Some humbler friend, my mortal journey done,
More near in blood, a Nephew or a Son,
In that dread hour Executor I'll leave;
For I, alas! have many to receive,
To give but little—To great GLOSTER *Health*;
Nor let thy true and proper love of wealth
Here take a false alarm—in purse though poor,
In spirit I'm right proud, nor can endure
The mention of a bribe—thy pocket's free,
I, though a Dedicator, scorn a fee.
Let thy own offspring all thy fortunes share;
I would not ALLEN rob, nor ALLEN'S heir.

   Think not, a Thought unworthy thy great' soul,
Which pomps of this world never could control,
Which never offered up at Power's vain shrine,
Think not that Pomp and Power can work on mine.
'Tis not thy Name, though that indeed is great,
'Tis not thy tinsel trumpery of state,
'Tis not thy Title, Doctor though thou art,
'Tis not thy Mitre, which hath won my heart.

State is a farce, Names are but empty Things,
Degrees are bought, and, by mistaken kings,
Titles are oft misplaced; Mitres, which shine
So bright in other eyes, are dull in mine,
Unless set off by Virtue; who deceives
Under the sacred sanction of *Lawn-Sleeves*,
Enhances guilt, commits a double sin;
So fair without, and yet so foul within.
'Tis not thy outward form, thy easy mien,
Thy sweet complacency, thy brow serene,
Thy open front, thy Love-commanding eye,
Where fifty Cupids, as in ambush, lie,
Which can from sixty to sixteen impart
The force of Love, and point his blunted dart;
'Tis not thy Face, though that by Nature's made
An Index to thy soul, though there displayed
We see thy mind at large, and through thy skin
Peeps out that Courtesy which dwells within;
'Tis not thy Birth—for that is low as mine,
Around our heads no lineal glories shine—
But what is Birth, when, to delight mankind,
Heralds can make those arms they cannot find;
When Thou art to Thyself, thy Sire unknown,
A Whole, Welch Genealogy *alone?*
No, 'tis thy inward Man, thy proper Worth,
Thy right just Estimation here on earth,
Thy Life and Doctrine uniformly joined,
And flowing from that wholesome source thy mind,
Thy known contempt of Persecution's rod,
Thy Charity for Man, thy Love of God,
Thy Faith in Christ, so well approved 'mongst men,
Which now give life, and utterance to my pen.
Thy Virtue, not thy Rank, demands my lays;
'Tis not the Bishop, but the Saint I praise.
Raised by that Theme, I soar on wings more strong,
And burst forth into praise withheld too long.

Much did I wish, e'en whilst I kept those sheep,
Which, for my curse, I was ordained to keep;
Ordained, alas! to keep through need, not choice,
Those sheep which never heard their shepherd's voice,
Which did not know, yet would not learn their way,
Which strayed themselves, yet grieved that I should stray,
Those sheep, which my good Father (on his bier

Let filial duty drop the pious tear)
Kept well, yet starved himself, e'en at that time,
Whilst I was pure, and innocent of rime,
Whilst, sacred Dullness ever in my view,
Sleep at my bidding crept from pew to pew,
Much did I wish, though little could I hope,
A Friend in him, who was the Friend of POPE.

His hand, said I, my youthful steps shall guide,
And lead me safe where thousands fall beside;
His Temper, his Experience shall control,
And hush to peace the tempest of my soul;
His Judgment teach me, from the Critic school,
How not to err, and how to err by rule;
Instruct me, mingling profit with delight,
Where POPE was wrong, where SHAKESPEARE was not right;
Where they are justly praised, and where through whim,
How little's due to them, how much to him.
Raised 'bove the slavery of common rules,
Of Commonsense, of modern, ancient schools,
Those feelings banished, which mislead us all,
Fools as we are, and which we Nature call,
He, by his great example, might impart
A better something, and baptize it Art;
He, all the feelings of my youth forgot,
Might show me what is Taste, by what is not;
By him supported, with a proper pride,
I might hold all mankind as fools beside;
He (should a World, perverse and peevish grown,
Explode his maxims, and assert their own)
Might teach me, like himself, to be content,
And let their folly be their punishment;
Might, like himself, teach his adopted Son,
'Gainst all the World, to quote a WARBURTON.

Fool that I was, could I so much deceive
My soul with lying hopes; could I believe
That He, the servant of his Maker sworn,
The servant of his Saviour, would be torn
From their embrace, and leave that dear employ,
The cure of souls, his duty and his joy,
For toys like mine, and waste his precious time,
On which so much depended, for a rime?
Should He forsake the task he undertook,
Desert his flock, and break his pastoral crook?

Should He (forbid it Heaven) so high in place,
So rich in knowledge, quit the work of Grace,
And, idly wandering o'er the Muses' hill,
Let the salvation of mankind stand still?

Far, far be that from Thee—yes, far from Thee
Be such revolt from Grace, and far from me
The Will to think it—Guilt is in the Thought—
Not so, Not so, hath WARBURTON been taught,
Not so learned Christ—Recall that day, well-known,
When (to maintain God's honor—and his own)
He called Blasphemers forth—Methinks I now
See stern Rebuke enthroned on his brow,
And armed with tenfold terrors—from his tongue,
Where fiery zeal, and Christian fury hung,
Methinks I hear the deep-toned thunders roll,
And chill with horror every sinner's soul—
In vain They strive to fly—flight cannot save,
And POTTER trembles even in his grave—
With all the conscious pride of innocence,
Methinks I hear him, in his own defense,
Bear witness to himself, whilst all Men knew,
By Gospel-rules, his witness to be true.

O Glorious Man, thy zeal I must commend,
Though it deprived me of my dearest friend.
The real motives of thy anger known,
WILKES must the justice of that anger own;
And, could thy bosom have been bared to view,
Pitied himself, in turn had pitied you.

Bred to the law, You wisely took the gown,
Which I, like *Demas*, foolishly laid down.
Hence double strength our *Holy Mother* drew;
Me she got rid of, and made prize of you.
I, like an idle Truant, fond of play,
Doting on toys, and throwing gems away,
Grasping at shadows, let the substance slip;
But you, *my Lord*, renounced Attorneyship
With better purpose, and more noble aim,
And wisely played a more substantial game.
Nor did *Law* mourn, blessed in her younger son,
For MANSFIELD does what GLOSTER would have done.

Doctor, Dean, Bishop, Gloster, and *My Lord*,
If haply these high Titles may accord
With thy meek Spirit, if the barren sound
Of pride delights Thee, to the topmost round
Of Fortune's ladder got, despise not One,
For want of smooth hypocrisy undone,
Who, far below, turns up his wondering eye,
And, without envy, sees Thee placed so high,
Let not thy Brain (as Brains less potent might)
Dizzy, confounded, giddy with the height,
Turn round, and lose distinction, lose her skill
And wonted powers of knowing good from ill,
Of sifting Truth from falsehood, friends from foes;
Let GLOSTER well remember, how he rose,
Nor turn his back on men who made him great;
Let Him not, gorged with power, and drunk with state,
Forget what once he was, though now so high;
How low, how mean, and full as poor as I.

Cetera desunt.

JONES VERY   (1813-1880)
American

The Hand and Foot

The hand and foot that stir not, they shall find
Sooner than all the rightful place to go:
Now in their motion free as roving wind,
Though first no snail so limited and slow;
I mark them full of labor all the day,
Each active motion made in perfect rest;
They cannot from their path mistaken stray,
Though 'tis not theirs, yet in it they are blest;
The bird has not their hidden track found out,
The cunning fox though full of art he .be;
It is the way unseen, the certain route,
Wherever bound, yet thou art ever free;
The path of Him, whose perfect law of love
Bids spheres and atoms in just order move.

Thy Brother's Blood

I have no brother. They who meet me now
Offer a hand with their own wills defiled,
And, while they wear a smooth unwrinkled brow,
Know not that Truth can never be beguiled.
Go wash the hand that still betrays thy guilt;—
Before the Spirit's gaze what stain can hide?
Abel's red blood upon the earth is spilt,
And by thy tongue it cannot be denied.
I hear not with the ear,—the heart doth tell
Its secret deeds to me untold before;
Go, all its hidden plunder quickly sell,
Then shalt thou cleanse thee from thy brother's gore,
Then will I take thy gift;—that bloody stain
Shall not be seen upon thy hand again.

The Lost

The fairest day that ever yet has shone,
Will be when thou the day within shalt see;
The fairest rose that ever yet has blown,
When thou the flower thou lookest on shalt be;
But thou art far away among Time's toys;
Thyself the day thou lookest for in them,
Thyself the flower that now thine eye enjoys,
But wilted now thou hang'st upon thy stem.
The bird thou hearest on the budding tree,
Thou hast made sing with thy forgotten voice;
But when it swells again to melody,
The song is thine in which thou wilt rejoice;
And thou new risen 'midst these wonders live
That now to them dost all thy substance give.

The Created

There is naught for thee by thy haste to gain;
'Tis not the swift with Me that win the race;
Through long endurance of delaying pain,
Thine opened eye shall see thy Father's face;
Nor here nor there, where now thy feet would turn,
Thou wilt find Him who ever seeks for thee;
But let obedience quench desires that burn,
And where thou art, thy Father too will be!
Behold! as day by day the spirit grows,
Thou see'st by inward light things hid before;
Till what God is, thyself His image shows;
And thou dost wear the robe that first thou wore,
When bright with radiance from his forming hand,
He saw thee lord of all His creatures stand.

FREDERICK GODDARD TUCKERMAN   (1821-1873)
American

from the Second Series

Elegy in Six Sonnets

XV
Gertrude and Gulielma, sister-twins,
Dwelt in the valley at the farmhouse old;
Nor grief had touched their locks of dark and gold
Nor dimmed the fragrant whiteness of their skins:
Both beautiful, and one in height and mould;
Yet one had loveliness which the spirit wins
To other worlds: eyes, forehead, smile and all,
More softly serious than the twilight's fall.
The other—can I e'er forget the day
When, stealing from a laughing group away,
To muse with absent eye and motion slow,
Her beauty fell upon me like a blow?—
Gertrude! with red flowerlip, and silk black hair!
Yet Gulielma was by far more fair.

XVI
Under the mountain, as when first I knew
Its low dark roof and chimney creeper-twined,
The red house stands; and yet my footsteps find,
Vague in the walks, waste balm and feverfew.
But they are gone: no soft-eyed sisters trip
Across the porch or lintels; where, behind,
The mother sat, sat knitting with pursed lip.
The house stands vacant in its green recess,
Absent of beauty as a broken heart.
The wild rain enters, and the sunset wind
Sighs in the chambers of their loveliness
Or shakes the pane—and in the silent noons
The glass falls from the window, part by part,
And ringeth faintly in the grassy stones.

XVII

Roll on, sad world! not Mercury or Mars
Could swifter speed, or slower, round the sun
Than in this year of variance thou hast done
To me: yet pain, fear, heart-break, woes and wars
Have natural limit; from his dread eclipse
The swift sun hastens, and the night debars
The day but to bring in the day more bright.
The flowers renew their odorous fellowships;
The moon runs round and round, the slow earth dips,
True to her poise, and lifts; the planet-stars
Roll and return from circle to ellipse;
The day is dull and soft, the eavetrough drips,
And yet I know the splendor of the light
Will break anon. Look! where the gray is white!

XVIII

And change with hurried hand has swept these scenes:
The woods have fallen, across the meadow-lot
The hunter's trail and trap-path is forgot,
And fire has drunk the swamps of evergreens;
Yet for a moment let my fancy plant
These autumn hills again: the wild dove's haunt,
The wild deer's walk. In golden umbrage shut,
The Indian river runs, Quonecktacut!
Here, but a lifetime back, where falls tonight
Behind the curtained pane a sheltered light
On buds of rose or vase of violet
Aloft upon the marble mantel set,
Here in the forest-heart, hung blackening
The wolfbait on the bush beside the spring.

XIX

And faces, forms and phantoms, numbered not,
Gather and pass like mist upon the breeze,
Jading the eye with uncouth images:
Women with muskets, children dropping shot
By fields half harvested or left in fear
Of Indian inroad, or the Hessian near;
Disaster, poverty, and dire disease.
Or from the burning village, through the trees
I see the smoke in reddening volumes roll,
The Indian file in shadowy silence pass
While the last man sets up the trampled grass,
The Tory priest declaiming, fierce and fat,
The Shay's man with the green branch in his hat,
Or silent sagamore, Shaug or Wassahoale.

XX

O hard endeavor, to blend in with these
Dark shadings of the past a darker grief
Or blur with stranger woes a wound so chief,
Though the great world turn slow with agonies.
What though the forest windflowers fell and died
And Gertrude sleeps at Gulielma's side?
They have their tears, nor turn to us their eyes:
But we pursue our dead with groans and cries
And bitter reclamations to the term
Of undiscerning darkness and the worm;
Then sit in silence down and darkly dwell
Through the slow years on all we loved, and tell
Each tone, each look of love, each syllable,
With lips that work, with eyes that overwell.

The Cricket

I

The humming bee purrs softly o'er his flower;
　　From lawn and thicket
The dogday locust singeth in the sun
　　From hour to hour:
Each has his bard, and thou, ere day be done,
　　Shalt have no wrong.
So bright that murmur mid the insect crowd,
Muffled and lost in bottom-grass, or loud
　　By pale and picket:
Shall I not take to help me in my song
　　A little cooing cricket?

II

The afternoon is sleepy; let us lie
Beneath these branches whilst the burdened brook,
Muttering and moaning to himself, goes by;
And mark our minstrel's carol whilst we look
Toward the faint horizon swooning blue.
　　Or in a garden bower,
Trellised and trammeled with deep drapery
　　Of hanging green,
　　Light glimmering through—
There let the dull hop be,
Let bloom, with poppy's dark refreshing flower:
Let the dead fragrance round our temples beat,
Stunning the sense to slumber, whilst between
The falling water and fluttering wind
　　Mingle and meet,
　　Murmer and mix,
No few faint pipings from the glades behind,
　　Or alder-thicks:
But louder as the day declines,
From tingling tassel, blade, and sheath,
Rising from nets of river vines,
　　Winrows and ricks,
　　Above, beneath,
　　At every breath,
At hand, around, illimitably
Rising and falling like the sea,
　　Acres of cricks!

III

Dear to the child who hears thy rustling voice
Cease at his footstep, though he hears thee still,
Cease and resume with vibrance crisp and shrill,
Thou sittest in the sunshine to rejoice.
Night lover too: bringer of all things dark
And rest and silence; yet thou bringest to me
Always that burthen of the unresting Sea,
The moaning cliffs, the low rocks blackly stark;
These upland inland fields no more I view,
But the long flat seaside beach, the wild seamew,
   And the overturning wave!
Thou bringest too, dim accents from the grave
To him who walketh when the day is dim,
Dreaming of those who dream no more of him,
With edged remembrances of joy and pain;
And heyday looks and laughter come again:
Forms that in happy sunshine lie and leap,
With faces where but now a gap must be,
Renunciations, and partitions deep
And perfect tears, and crowning vacancy!
And to thy poet at the twilight's hush,
No chirping touch of lips with laugh and blush,
But wringing arms, hearts wild with love and woe,
Closed eyes, and kisses that would not let go!

IV

So wert thou loved in that old graceful time
   When Greece was fair,
While god and hero hearkened to thy chime;
   Softly astir
Where the long grasses fringed Cayster's lip;
Long-drawn, with glimmering sails of swan and ship,
   And ship and swan;
   Or where
   Reedy Eurotas ran.
Did that low warble teach thy tender flute
   Xenaphyle?

Its breathings mild? say! did the grasshopper
Sit golden in thy purple hair
   O Psammathe?
   Or wert thou mute,
Grieving for Pan amid the alders there?
And by the water and along the hill
That thirsty tinkle in the herbage still,
Though the lost forest wailed to horns of Arcady?

V

Like the Enchanter old—
Who sought mid the dead water's weeds and scum
For evil growths beneath the moonbeam cold,
   Or mandrake or dorcynium;
And touched the leaf that opened both his ears,
So that articulate voices now he hears
In cry of beast, or bird, or insect's hum,—
Might I but find thy knowledge in thy song!
   That twittering tongue,
Ancient as light, returning like the years.
   So might I be,
Unwise to sing, thy true interpreter
Through denser stillness and in sounder dark,
Than ere thy notes have pierced to harrow me.
   So might I stir
   The world to hark
   To thee my lord and lawgiver,
   And cease my quest:
Content to bring thy wisdom to the world;
Content to gain at last some low applause,
   Now low, now lost
Like thine from mossy stone, amid the stems and straws,
   Or garden gravemound tricked and dressed—
   Powdered and pearled
   By stealing frost—
In dusky rainbow beauty of euphorbias!
For larger would be less indeed, and like
The ceaseless simmer in the summer grass
To him who toileth in the windy field,
   Or where the sunbeams strike,
Naught in innumerable numerousness.

So might I much possess,
So much must yield;
But failing this, the dell and grassy dike,
The water and the waste shall still be dear,
And all the pleasant plots and places
    Where thou hast sung, and I have hung
    To ignorantly hear.
Then Cricket, sing thy song! or answer mine!
Thine whispers blame, but mine has naught but praises.
It matters not. Behold! the autumn goes,
    The shadow grows,
The moments take hold of eternity;
Even while we stop to wrangle or repine
    Our lives are gone—
    Like thinnest mist,
Like yon escaping color in the tree;
Rejoice! rejoice! whilst yet the hours exist—
Rejoice or mourn, and let the world swing on
Unmoved by cricket song of thee or me.

from the Fifth Series

Sonnet XIV

And me my winter's task is drawing over,
Though night and winter shake the drifted door.
Critic or friend, dispraiser or approver,
I come not now nor fain would offer more.
But when buds break and round the fallen limb
The wild weeds crowd in clusters and corymb,
When twilight rings with the red robin's plaint,
Let me give something—though my heart be faint—
To thee, my more than friend!—believer! lover!
The gust has fallen now, and all is mute—
Save pricking on the pane the sleety showers,
The clock that ticks like a belated foot,
Time's hurrying step, the twanging of the hours:
Wait for those days, my friend, or get thee fresher flowers.

EMILY DICKINSON* (1830-1886)
American

Farther in summer than the birds

Farther in summer than the birds,
Pathetic from the grass,
A minor nation celebrates
Its unobtrusive mass.

No ordinance is seen,
So gradual the grace,
A pensive custom it becomes,
Enlarging loneliness.

Antiquest felt at noon
When August, burning low,
Calls forth this spectral canticle,
Repose to typify.

Remit as yet no grace,
No furrow on the glow,
Yet a druidic difference
Enhances nature now.

As imperceptibly as grief

As imperceptibly as grief
The summer lapsed away,—
Too imperceptible, at last,
To seem like perfidy.

A quietness distilled,
As twilight long begun,
Or Nature, spending with herself
Sequestered afternoon.

The dusk drew earlier in,
The morning foreign shone,—
A courteous, yet harrowing grace,
As guest who would be gone.

And thus, without a wing,
Or service of a keel,
Our summer made her light escape
Into the beautiful.

There's a certain slant of light

There's a certain slant of light,
On winter afternoons,
That oppresses, like the weight
Of cathedral tunes.

Heavenly hurt it gives us;
We can find no scar,
But internal difference
Where the meanings are.

None may teach it anything,
'Tis the seal, despair,—
An imperial affliction
Sent us of the air.

When it comes, the landscape listens,
Shadows hold their breath;
When it goes, 'tis like the distance
On the look of death.

The last night that she lived

The last night that she lived
It was a common night,
Except the dying; this to us
Made nature different.

We waited while she passed;
It was a narrow time,
Too jostled were our souls to speak,
At length the notice came.

She mentioned, and forgot;
Then lightly as a reed
Bent to the water, shivered scarce,
Consented, and was dead.

And we, we placed the hair,
And drew the head erect;
And then an awful leisure was,
Our faith to regulate.

I read my sentence steadily

I read my sentence steadily,
Reviewed it with my eyes,
To see that I made no mistake
In its extremest clause,—

I made my soul familiar
With her extremity,
That at the last it should not be
A novel agony,

But she and Death, acquainted,
Meet tranquilly as friends,
Salute and pass without a hint—
And there the matter ends.

Our journey had advanced

Our journey had advanced;
Our feet were almost come
To that odd fork in Being's road,
Eternity by term.

Our pace took sudden awe,
Our feet reluctant led.
Before were cities, but between,
The forest of the dead.

Retreat was out of hope,—
Behind, a sealéd route,
Eternity's white flag before,
And God at every gate.

The difference between despair

The difference between despair
And fear, is like the one
Between the instant of a wreck,
And when the wreck has been.

The mind is smooth,—no motion—
Contented as the eye
Upon the forehead of a Bust,
That knows it cannot see.

The Moon upon her fluent route

The Moon upon her fluent route
Defiant of a road,
The Stars Etruscan argument,
Substantiate a God.
If Aims impel these Astral Ones,
The Ones allowed to know
Know that which makes them as forgot
As Dawn forgets them now.

'Twas warm at first like us

'Twas warm at first like us,
Until there crept thereon
A chill, like frost upon a glass,
Till all the scene be gone.

The forehead copied stone,
The fingers grew too cold
To ache, and like a skater's brook
The busy eyes congealed.

It straightened—that was all—
It crowded cold to cold—
It multiplied indifference
As Pride were all it could.

And even when with cords
'Twas lowered like a freight,
It made no signal, nor demurred,
But dropped like adamant.

---

*For all of these poems except *'Twas warm at first*, we have used the versions first published by Mabel Loomis Todd; for this one poem we have used the version first published by Martha Dickinson Bianchi and Alfred Leete Hampson in *Further Poems of Emily Dickinson*, 1921. We have omitted three stanzas, however, which are bad in themselves and do not advance the poems: two and three from *The last night* and two from *I read my sentence*.

THOMAS HARDY (1840-1928)

I Say I'll Seek Her

I say, "I'll seek her side
  Ere hindrance interposes;"
  But eve in midnight closes,
And here I still abide.

When darkness wears I see
  Her sad eyes in a vision;
  They ask, "What indecision
Detains you, Love, from me?—

"The creaking hinge is oiled,
  I have unbarred the backway,
  But you tread not the trackway
And shall the thing be spoiled?

"Far cockcrows echo shrill,
  The shadows are abating,
  And I am waiting, waiting;
But O, you tarry still!"

"My Spirit Will Not Haunt the Mound"

My spirit will not haunt the mound
  Above my breast,
But travel, memory-possessed,
To where my tremulous being found
  Life largest, best.

My phantom-footed shape will go
  When nightfall grays
Hither and thither along the ways
I and another used to know
  In backward days.

And there you'll find me, if a jot
  You still should care
For me, and for my curious air;
If otherwise, then I shall not,
  For you, be there.

The Haunter

He does not think that I haunt here nightly:
   How shall I let him know
That whither his fancy sets him wandering
   I, too, alertly go?—
Hover and hover a few feet from him
   Just as I used to do,
But cannot answer the words he lifts me—
   Only listen thereto!

When I could answer he did not say them:
   When I could let him know
How I would like to join in his journeys
   Seldom he wished to go.
Now that he goes and wants me with him
   More than he used to do,
Never he sees my faithful phantom
   Though he speaks thereto.

Yes, I companion him to places
   Only dreamers know,
Where the shy hares print long paces,
   Where the night rooks go;
Into old aisles where the past is all to him
   Close as his shade can do,
Always lacking the power to call to him,
   Near as I reach thereto!

What a good haunter I am, O tell him!
   Quickly make him know
If he but sigh since my loss befell him
   Straight to his side I go.
Tell him a faithful one is doing
   All that love can do
Still that his path may be worth pursuing,
   And to bring peace thereto.

Exeunt Omnes

I

   Everybody else, then, going,
And I still left where the fair was? . . .
Much have I seen of neighbor loungers
   Making a lusty showing,
   Each now past all knowing.

II

   There is an air of blankness
In the street and the littered spaces;
Thoroughfare, steeple, bridge and highway
   Wizen themselves to lankness;
   Kennels dribble dankness.

III

   Folk all fade. And whither,
As I wait alone where the fair was?
Into the clammy and numbing night-fog
   Whence they entered hither.
   Soon one more goes thither!

The Faded Face

How was this I did not see
Such a look as here was shown
Ere its womanhood had blown
Past its first felicity?—
That I did not know you young
   Faded Face,
      Know you young!

Why did Time so ill bestead
That I heard no voice of yours
Hail from out the curved contours
Of those lips when rosy red;
Weeted not the songs they sung,
   Faded Face,
      Songs they sung!

By these blanchings, blooms of old,
And the relics of your voice—
Leavings rare of rich and choice
From your early tone and mould—
Let me mourn,—aye, sorrow-wrung.
   Faded Face,
      Sorrow-wrung!

During Wind and Rain

    They sing their dearest songs—
    He, she, all of them—yea,
    Treble and tenor and bass,
       And one to play;
    With the candles mooning each face. ...
       Ah, no; the years O!
How the sick leaves reel down in throngs!

    They clear the creeping moss—
    Elders and juniors—aye,
    Making the pathways neat
       And the garden gay;
    And they build a shady seat. ...
       Ah, no; the years, the years;
See, the white storm-birds wing across!

    They are blithely breakfasting all—
    Men and maidens—yea,
    Under the summer tree,
       With a glimpse of the bay,
    While pet fowl come to the knee. ...
       Ah, no; the years O!
And the rotten rose is ript from the wall.

    They change to a high new house,
    He, she, all of them—aye,
    Clocks and carpets and chairs
       On the lawn all day,
    And brightest things that are theirs. ...
       Ah, no; the years, the years;
Down their carved names the rain-drop ploughs.

"Who's in the Next Room?"

"Who's in the next room?—who?
    I seemed to see
Somebody in the dawning passing through,
    Unknown to me."
"Nay: you saw nought. He passed invisibly."

"Who's in the next room?—who?
    I seem to hear
Somebody muttering firm in a language new
    That chills the ear."
"No: you catch not his tongue who has entered there."

"Who's in the next room?—who?
    I seem to feel
His breath like a clammy draught, as if it drew
    From the Polar Wheel."
"No: none who breathes at all does the door conceal."

"Who's in the next room?—who?
    A figure wan
With a message to one in there of something due?
    Shall I know him anon?"
"Yea he; and he brought such; and you'll know him anon."

The Shadow on the Stone

    I went by the Druid stone
  That broods in the garden white and lone,
And I stopped and looked at the shifting shadows
  That at some moments fall thereon
  From the tree hard by with a rhythmic swing,
  And they shaped in my imagining
To the shade that a well-known head and shoulders
  Threw there when she was gardening.

    I thought her behind my back,
  Yea, her I long had learned to lack,
And I said: "I am sure you are standing behind me,
  Though how do you get into this old track?"
  And there was no sound but the fall of a leaf
  As a sad response; and to keep down grief
I would not turn my head to discover
  That there was nothing in my belief.

    Yet I wanted to look and see
  That nobody stood at the back of me;
But I thought once more: "Nay, I'll not unvision
  A shape which, somehow, there may be."
  So I went on softly from the glade,
  And left her behind me throwing her shade,
As she were indeed an apparition—
  My head unturned lest my dream should fade.

In Time of "The Breaking of Nations"

I

Only a man harrowing clods
   In a slow silent walk
With an old horse that stumbles and nods
   Half asleep as they stalk.

II

Only thin smoke without flame
   From the heaps of couch-grass;
Yet this will go onward the same
   Though Dynasties pass.

III

Yonder a maid and her wight
   Come whispering by:
War's annals will cloud into night
   Ere their story die.

Afterwards

When the Present has latched its postern behind my
    tremulous stay,
  And the May month flaps its glad green leaves like wings,
Delicate-filmed as new-spun silk, will the neighbors say,
    "He was a man who used to notice such things"?

If it be in the dusk when, like an eyelid's soundless blink,
  The dewfall-hawk comes crossing the shades to alight
Upon the wind-warped upland thorn, a gazer may think,
    "To him this must have been a familiar sight."

If I pass during some nocturnal blackness, mothy and warm,
  When the hedgehog travels furtively over the lawn,
One may say, "He strove that such innocent creatures should
    come to no harm,
    But he could do little for them; and now he is gone."

If, when hearing that I have been stilled at last, they
    stand at the door,
  Watching the full-starred heavens that winter sees,
Will this thought rise on those who will meet my face no more,
    "He was one who had an eye for such mysteries"?

And will any say when my bell of quittance is heard in the
    gloom,
  And a crossing breeze cuts a pause in its outrollings,
Till they rise again, as they were a new bell's boom,
    "He hears it not now, but used to notice such things"?

Dejection

Wherefore tonight so full of care,
My soul, revolving hopeless strife,
Pointing at hindrance, and the bare
Painful escapes of fitful life?

Shaping the doom that may befall
By precedent of terror past:
By love dishonored, and the call
Of friendship slighted at the last?

By treasured names, the little store
That memory out of wreck could save
Of loving hearts, that gone before
Call their old comrade to the grave?

   O soul, be patient: thou shalt find
A little matter mend all this;
Some strain of music to thy mind,
Some praise for skill not spent amiss.

Again shall pleasure overflow
Thy cup with sweetness, thou shalt taste
Nothing but sweetness, and shalt grow
Half sad for sweetness run to waste.

O happy life! I hear thee sing,
O rare delight of mortal stuff!
I praise my days for all they bring,
Yet are they only not enough.

The Affliction of Richard

Love not too much. But how,
When thou hast made me such,
And dost thy gifts bestow,
How can I love too much?
    Though I must fear to lose,
And drown my joy in care,
With all its thorns I choose
The path of love and prayer.

    Though thou, I know not why,
Didst kill my childish trust,
That breach with toil did I
Repair, because I must:
    And spite of frighting schemes,
With which the fiends of Hell
Blaspheme thee in my dreams,
So far I have hoped well.

    But what the heavenly key,
What marvel in me wrought
Shall quite exculpate thee,
I have no shadow of thought.
    What am I that complain?
The love, from which began
My question sad and vain,
Justifies thee to man.

Eros

Why hast thou nothing in thy face?
Thou idol of the human race,
Thou tyrant of the human heart,
The flower of lovely youth that art;
Yea, and that standest in thy youth
An image of eternal Truth,
With thy exuberant flesh so fair,
That only Pheidias might compare,
Ere from his chaste marmoreal form
Time had decayed the colors warm;
Like to his gods in thy proud dress,
Thy starry sheen of nakedness.

Surely thy body is thy mind,
For in thy face is nought to find,
Only thy soft unchristen'd smile,
That shadows neither love nor guile,
But shameless will and power immense,
In secret sensuous innocence.

O king of joy, what is thy thought?
I dream thou knowest it is nought,
And wouldst in darkness come, but thou
Makest the light where'er thou go.
Ah yet no victim of thy grace,
None who e'er long'd for thy embrace,
Hath cared to look upon thy face.

Low Barometer

The south-wind strengthens to a gale,
Across the moon the clouds fly fast,
The house is smitten as with a flail,
The chimney shudders to the blast.

On such a night, when Air has loosed
Its guardian grasp on blood and brain,
Old terrors then of god or ghost
Creep from their caves to life again;

And Reason kens he herits in
A haunted house. Tenants unknown
Assert their squalid lease of sin
With earlier title than his own.

Unbodied presences, the packed
Pollution and remorse of Time,
Slipped from oblivion reenact
The horrors of unhouseld crime.

Some men would quell the thing with prayer
Whose sightless footsteps pad the floor,
Whose fearful trespass mounts the stair
Or bursts the locked forbidden door.

Some have seen corpses long interred
Escape from hallowing control,
Pale charnel forms—nay ev'n have heard
The shrilling of a troubled soul,

That wanders till the dawn hath crossed
The dolorous dark, or Earth hath wound
Closer her storm-spredd cloak, and thrust
The baleful phantoms underground.

Ἐτώσιον ἄχθος ἀρούρης

Who goes there? God knows. I'm nobody. How should I answer?
    Can't jump over a gate nor run across the meadow.
I'm but an old whitebeard of inane identity. Pass on!
    What's left of me today will very soon be nothing.

AGNES LEE   (1868-1939)
American

The Sweeper

Frail, wistful guardian of the broom,
The dwelling's drudge and stay,
Whom destiny gave a single task—
To keep the dust away!

Sweep off the floor and polish the chair.
It will not always last.
Some day, for all your arms can do,
The dust will hold you fast.

EDWIN ARLINGTON ROBINSON   (1869-1935)
American

Eros Turannos

She fears him, and will always ask
    What fated her to choose him;
She meets in his engaging mask
    All reasons to refuse him;
But what she meets and what she fears
Are less than are the downward years,
Drawn slowly to the foamless weirs
    Of age, were she to lose him.

Between a blurred sagacity
    That once had power to sound him,
And Love, that will not let him be
    The Judas that she found him,
Her pride assuages her almost,
As if it were alone the cost.—
He sees that he will not be lost,
    And waits and looks around him.

A sense of ocean and old trees
    Envelops and allures him;
Tradition, touching all he sees,
    Beguiles and reassures him;
And all her doubts of what he says
Are dimmed with what she knows of days—
Till even prejudice delays
    And fades, and she secures him.

The falling leaf inaugurates
   The reign of her confusion;
The pounding wave reverberates
   The dirge of her illusion;
And home, where passion lived and died,
Becomes a place where she can hide,
While all the town and harbor side
   Vibrate with her seclusion.

We tell you, tapping on our brows,
   The story as it should be,—
As if the story of a house
   Were told, or ever could be;
We'll have no kindly veil between
Her visions and those we have seen,—
As if we guessed what hers have been,
   Or what they are or would be.

Meanwhile we do no harm; for they
   That with a god have striven,
Not hearing much of what we say,
   Take what the god has given;
Though like waves breaking it may be
Or like a changed familiar tree,
Or like a stairway to the sea
   Where down the blind are driven.

Veteran Sirens

The ghost of Ninon would be sorry now
To laugh at them, were she to see them here,
So brave and so alert for learning how
To fence with reason for another year.

Age offers a far comelier diadem
Than theirs; but anguish has no eye for grace,
When time's malicious mercy cautions them
To think a while of number and of space.

The burning hope, the worn expectancy,
The martyred humor, and the maimed allure,
Cry out for time to end his levity,
And age to soften its investiture;

But they, though others fade and are still fair,
Defy their fairness and are unsubdued;
Although they suffer, they may not forswear
The patient ardor of the unpursued.

Poor flesh, to fight the calendar so long;
Poor vanity, so quaint and yet so brave;
Poor folly, so deceived and yet so strong,
So far from Ninon and so near the grave.

Luke Havergal

Go to the western gate, Luke Havergal,
There where the vines cling crimson on the wall,
And in the twilight wait for what will come.
The leaves will whisper there of her, and some,
Like flying words, will strike you as they fall;
But go, and if you listen she will call.
Go to the western gate, Luke Havergal—
Luke Havergal.

No, there is not a dawn in eastern skies
To rift the fiery night that's in your eyes;
But there, where western glooms are gathering,
The dark will end the dark, if anything:
God slays Himself with every leaf that flies,
And hell is more than half of paradise.
No, there is not a dawn in eastern skies—
In eastern skies.

Out of a grave I come to tell you this,
Out of a grave I come to quench the kiss
That flames upon your forehead with a glow
That blinds you to the way that you must go.
Yes, there is yet one way to where she is,
Bitter, but one that faith may never miss.
Out of a grave I come to tell you this—
To tell you this.

There is the western gate, Luke Havergal,
There are the crimson leaves upon the wall.
Go, for the winds are tearing them away,—
Nor think to riddle the dead words they say,
Nor any more to feel them as they fall;
But go, and if you trust her she will call.
There is the western gate, Luke Havergal—
Luke Havergal.

The Wandering Jew

I saw by looking in his eyes
That they remembered everything;
And this was how I came to know
That he was here, still wandering.
For though the figure and the scene
Were never to be reconciled,
I knew the man as I had known
His image when I was a child.

With evidence at every turn,
I should have held it safe to guess
That all the newness of New York
Had nothing new in loneliness;
Yet here was one who might be Noah,
Or Nathan, or Abimelech,
Or Lamech, out of ages lost,—
Or, more than all, Melchizedek.

Assured that he was none of these,
I gave them back their names again,
To scan once more those endless eyes
Where all my questions ended then.
I found in them what they revealed
That I shall not live to forget,
And wondered if they found in mine
Compassion that I might regret.

Pity, I learned, was not the least
Of time's offending benefits
That had now for so long impugned
The conservation of his wits:
Rather it was that I should yield,
Alone, the fealty that presents
The tribute of a tempered ear
To an untempered eloquence.

Before I pondered long enough
On whence he came and who he was,
I trembled at his ringing wealth
Of manifold anathemas;
I wondered, while he seared the world,
What new defection ailed the race,
And if it mattered how remote
Our fathers were from such a place.

Before there was an hour for me
To contemplate with less concern
The crumbling realm awaiting us
Than his that was beyond return,
A dawning on the dust of years
Had shaped with an elusive light
Mirages of remembered scenes
That were no longer for the sight.

For now the gloom that hid the man
Became a daylight on his wrath,
And one wherein my fancy viewed
New lions ramping in his path.
The old were dead and had no fangs,
Wherefore he loved them—seeing not
They were the same that in their time
Had eaten everything they caught.

The world around him was a gift
Of anguish to his eyes and ears,
And one that he had long reviled
As fit for devils, not for seers.
Where, then, was there a place for him
That on this other side of death
Saw nothing good, as he had seen
No good come out of Nazareth?

Yet here there was a reticence,
And I believe his only one,
That hushed him as if he beheld
A Presence that would not be gone.
In such a silence he confessed
How much there was to be denied;
And he would look at me and live,
As others might have looked and died.

As if at last he knew again
That he had always known, his eyes
Were like to those of one who gazed
On those of One who never dies.
For such a moment he revealed
What life has in it to be lost;
And I could ask if what I saw
Before me there, was man or ghost.

He may have died so many times
That all there was of him to see
Was pride, that kept itself alive
As too rebellious to be free;
He may have told, when more than once
Humility seemed imminent,
How many a lonely time in vain
The Second Coming came and went.

Whether he still defies or not
The failure of an angry task
That relegates him out of time
To chaos, I can only ask.
But as I knew him, so he was;
And somewhere among men to-day
Those old, unyielding eyes may flash
And flinch—and look the other way.

T. STURGE MOORE   (1870-1944)

Silence

No word, no lie, can cross a carven lip;
No thought is quick behind a chiselled brow;
Speech is the cruel flaw in comradeship,
Whose self-bemusing ease daunts like a blow
Though unintended, irrevocable!
For wound, a mere quip dealt, no salve is found
Though poet be bled dry of words to tell
Why it was pointed! how it captured sound!
Charmed by mere phrases, we first glean their sense
When we behold our Helen streaming tears.
Give me dry eyes whose gaze but looks intense!
The dimpled lobes of unreceptive ears!
A statue not a heart! Silence so kind,
It answers love with beauty cleansed of mind.

From Titian's "Bacchanal" in the Prado at Madrid

She naked lies asleep beside the wine
That in a rill wanders through moss and flowers;
Her head thrown, and her hair, back o'er an urn
Whose metal glints from under crimpled gold
Of lately bound-up locks; while her flushed face
Breathes up toward open sky with fast-closed lids,—
As though, half-conscious, her complexion knew
Where stirred the tree-tops, where the blue was vast.
One arm, wrapped in a soft white crumpled vest,
An empty wine-dish guards; her breasts are young;
Young, although massive, torso, loins and thighs,
All hued as clouds are that the morning face.
Beside her foot three shadowed blue flowers glow,
Speedwell, or gentian, or some now lost gem
That then was found in Crete; some gem now lost,
Some precious flower, that then endeared the isles
To hearts of travelling gods and sailor princes.
Though friends of such an one here revel now,
And laugh, carouse, and dance, she hears them not;
Brown satyrs, maenads, men, these sing; and hark!
Birds sing, the sea is sighing, and the woods
Do sound as lovers love to hear them:—Sleep,
Sleep, oh! and wake no more; Bacchus has kissed
Thy lips, thine eyes, thy brow; thy joy and his
But lately were as one, therefore sleep on:
Be all past woes forgotten in thy dream!

This noisy crew still haunts thee;—but unheard
They sing, and birds are singing; thou dost sleep:
These dance, carouse, and pledge each other's joy;
Slowly the tree-tops, in the wind's embrace,
Dance too; lush branches and gay vestures float,
Float, wave and rustle, sighing to the wind;
But thou art still; thou sleepest, art divine.
Upon the purple clusters, in his drowse,
The vast Silenus rolls; and through the grass
The red juice trickles, forming rills and streams;
Comes down cascading, prattles past thy couch,
And winds on sea-ward; thou remainest, thou,
Perfectly still remainest and dost sleep.
These soon will leave thee,—satyr, maenad, faun,
Light-hearted young folk,—these will never stay
Past sundown nor out-watch the pale long eve,
But troop afar with fainter riot and song.
Then, when thou art alone and the wind dropped,
When the night finds thee, mayst thou still be sleeping:
She then, forever and for aye, will take thee
To her deep dwelling and unechoing halls;
How could she leave thee? she who owns them all—
Owns all the stars, whose beauty is complete,
Whose joy is perfect, and whose home is peace;
While all their duty is to shine for love.

ADELAIDE CRAPSEY   (1878-1914)
American

Snow

Look up . . .
From bleakening hills
Blows down the light, first breath
Of wintry wind . . . look up, and scent
The snow!

Night Winds

The old
Old winds that blew
When chaos was, what do
They tell the clattered trees that I
Should weep?

Roma Aeterna

The sun
Is warm to-day,
O Romulus, and on
Thine olden Palatine the birds
Still sing.

Amaze

I know
Not these my hands
And yet I think there was
A woman like me once had hands
Like these.

For Lucas Cranach's Eve

Ah me,
Was there a time
When Paradise knew Eve
In this sweet guise, so placid and
So young?

*To Man Who Goes Seeking Immortality, Bidding Him
   Look Nearer Home*

Too far afield thy search. Nay, turn. Nay, turn.
   At thine own elbow potent Memory stands,
Thy double, and eternity is cupped
   In the pale hollow of those ghostly hands.

WALLACE STEVENS   (1879-1955)
American

The Snow Man

One must have a mind of winter
To regard the frost and the boughs
Of the pine-trees crusted with snow;

And have been cold a long time
To behold the junipers shagged with ice,
The spruces rough in the distant glitter

Of the January sun; and not to think
Of any misery in the sound of the wind,
In the sound of a few leaves,

Which is the sound of the land
Full of the same wind
That is blowing in the same bare place

For the listener, who listens in the snow,
And, nothing himself, beholds
Nothing that is not there and the nothing that is.

On the Manner of Addressing Clouds

Gloomy grammarians in golden gowns,
Meekly you keep the mortal rendezvous,
Eliciting the still sustaining pomps
Of speech which are like music so profound
They seem an exaltation without sound.
Funest philosophers and ponderers,
Their evocations are the speech of clouds.
So speech of your processionals returns
In the casual evocations of your tread
Across the stale, mysterious seasons. These
Are the music of meet resignation; these
The responsive, still sustaining pomps for you
To magnify, if in that drifting waste
You are to be accompanied by more
Than mute bare splendors of the sun and moon.

Of Heaven Considered as a Tomb

What word have you, interpreters, of men
Who in the tomb of heaven walk by night,
The darkened ghosts of our old comedy?
Do they believe they range the gusty cold,
With lanterns borne aloft to light the way,
Freemen of death, about and still about
To find whatever it is they seek? Or does
That burial, pillared up each day as porte
And spiritous passage into nothingness,
Foretell each night the one abysmal night,
When the host shall no more wander, nor the light
Of the steadfast lanterns creep across the dark?
Make hue among the dark comedians,
Halloo them in the topmost distances,
For answer from their icy Élysée.

Sunday Morning

I

Complacencies of the peignoir, and late
Coffee and oranges in a sunny chair,
And the green freedom of a cockatoo
Upon a rug mingle to dissipate
The holy hush of ancient sacrifice.
She dreams a little, and she feels the dark
Encroachment of that old catastrophe,
As a calm darkens among water-lights.
The pungent oranges and bright, green wings
Seem things in some procession of the dead,
Winding across wide water, without sound.
The day is like wide water, without sound,
Stilled for the passing of her dreaming feet
Over the seas, to silent Palestine,
Dominion of the blood and sepulchre.

II

Why should she give her bounty to the dead?
What is divinity if it can come
Only in silent shadows and in dreams?
Shall she not find in comforts of the sun,
In pungent fruit and bright, green wings, or else
In any balm or beauty of the earth,
Things to be cherished like the thought of heaven?
Divinity must live within herself:
Passions of rain, or moods in falling snow;
Grievings in loneliness, or unsubdued
Elations when the forest blooms; gusty
Emotions on wet roads on autumn nights;
All pleasures and all pains, remembering
The bough of summer and the winter branch.
These are the measures destined for her soul.

III

Jove in the clouds had his inhuman birth.
No mother suckled him, no sweet land gave
Large-mannered motions to his mythy mind.
He moved among us, as a muttering king,
Magnificent, would move among his hinds,
Until our blood, commingling, virginal,
With heaven, brought such requital to desire
The very hinds discerned it, in a star.
Shall our blood fail? Or shall it come to be
The blood of paradise? And shall the earth
Seem all of paradise that we shall know?
The sky will be much friendlier then than now,
A part of labor and a part of pain,
And next in glory to enduring love,
Not this dividing and indifferent blue.

IV

She says, "I am content when wakened birds,
Before they fly, test the reality
Of misty fields, by their sweet questionings;
But when the birds are gone, and their warm fields
Return no more, where, then, is paradise?"
There is not any haunt of prophecy,
Nor any old chimera of the grave,
Neither the golden underground, nor isle
Melodious, where spirits gat them home,
Nor visionary south, nor cloudy palm
Remote on heaven's hill, that has endured
As April's green endures; or will endure
Like her remembrance of awakened birds,
Or her desire for June and evening, tipped
By the consummation of the swallow's wings.

V

She says, "But in contentment I still feel
The need of some imperishable bliss."
Death is the mother of beauty; hence from her
Alone, shall come fulfilment to our dreams
And our desires. Although she strews the leaves
Of sure obliteration on our paths,
The path sick sorrow took, the many paths
Where triumph rang its brassy phrase, or love
Whispered a little out of tenderness,
She makes the willow shiver in the sun
For maidens who were wont to sit and gaze
Upon the grass, relinquished to their feet.
She causes boys to pile new plums and pears
On disregarded plate. The maidens taste
And stray impassioned in the littering leaves.

VI

Is there no change of death in paradise?
Does ripe fruit never fall? Or do the boughs
Hang always heavy in that perfect sky,
Unchanging, yet so like our perishing earth,
With rivers like our own that seek for seas
They never find, the same receding shores
That never touch with inarticulate pang?
Why set the pear upon those river-banks
Or spice the shores with odors of the plum?
Alas, that they should wear our colors there,
The silken weavings of our afternoons,
And pick the strings of our insipid lutes!
Death is the mother of beauty, mystical,
Within whose burning bosom we devise
Our earthly mothers waiting, sleeplessly.

VII

Supple and turbulent, a ring of men
Shall chant in orgy on a summer morn
Their boisterous devotion to the sun,
Not as a god, but as a god might be,
Naked among them, like a savage source.
Their chant shall be a chant of paradise,
Out of their blood, returning to the sky;
And in their chant shall enter, voice by voice,
The windy lake wherein their lord delights,
The trees, like serafin, and echoing hills,
That choir among themselves long afterward.
They shall know well the heavenly fellowship
Of men that perish and of summer morn.
And whence they came and whither they shall go
The dew upon their feet shall manifest.

VIII

She hears, upon that water without sound,
A voice that cries, "The tomb in Palestine
Is not the porch of spirits lingering.
It is the grave of Jesus, where he lay."
We live in an old chaos of the sun,
Or old dependency of day and night,
Or island solitude, unsponsored, free,
Of that wide water, inescapable.
Deer walk upon our mountains, and the quail
Whistle about us their spontaneous cries;
Sweet berries ripen in the wilderness;
And, in the isolation of the sky,
At evening, casual flocks of pigeons make
Ambiguous undulations as they sink,
Downward to darkness, on extended wings.

The Death of a Soldier

Life contracts and death is expected,
As in a season of autumn.
The soldier falls.

He does not become a three-days personage,
Imposing his separation,
Calling for pomp.

Death is absolute and without memorial,
As in a season of autumn,
When the wind stops,

When the wind stops and, over the heavens,
The clouds go, nevertheless,
In their direction.

The Course of a Particular

Today the leaves cry, hanging on branches swept by wind,
Yet the nothingness of winter becomes a little less.
It is still full of icy shades and shapen snow.

The leaves cry . . . One holds off and merely hears the cry.
It is a busy cry, concerning someone else.
And though one says that one is part of everything,

There is a conflict, there is a resistance involved;
And being part is an exertion that declines:
One feels the life of that which gives life as it is.

The leaves cry. It is not a cry of divine attention,
Nor the smoke-drift of puffed-out heroes, nor human cry.
It is the cry of leaves that do not transcend themselves,

In the absence of fantasia, without meaning more
Than they are in the final finding of the ear, in the thing
Itself, until, at last, the cry concerns no one at all.

Complaint

They call me and I go.
It is a frozen road
past midnight, a dust
of snow caught
in the rigid wheeltracks.
The door opens.
I smile, enter and
shake off the cold.
Here is a great woman
on her side in the bed.
She is sick,
perhaps vomiting,
perhaps laboring
to give birth to
a tenth child. Joy! Joy!
Night is a room
darkened for lovers,
through the jalousies the sun
has sent one gold needle!
I pick the hair from her eyes
and watch her misery
with compassion.

To Waken an Old Lady

Old age is
a flight of small
cheeping birds
skimming
bare trees
above a snow glaze.
Gaining and failing
they are buffeted
by a dark wind—
But what?
On harsh weedstalks
the flock has rested,
the snow
is covered with broken
seedhusks
and the wind tempered
by a shrill
piping of plenty.

The Great Figure

Among the rain
and lights
I saw the figure 5
in gold
on a red
firetruck
moving
tense
unheeded
to gong clangs
siren howls
and wheels rumbling
through the dark city.

Spring and All

By the road to the contagious hospital
under the surge of the blue
mottled clouds driven from the
northeast—a cold wind. Beyond, the
waste of broad, muddy fields
brown with dried weeds, standing and fallen

patches of standing water
the scattering of tall trees

All along the road the reddish
purplish, forked, upstanding, twiggy
stuff of bushes and small trees
with dead, brown leaves under them
leafless vines—

Lifeless in appearance, sluggish
dazed spring approaches—

They enter the new world naked,
cold, uncertain of all
save that they enter. All about them
the cold, familiar wind—

Now the grass, tomorrow
the stiff curl of wildcarrot leaf
One by one objects are defined—
It quickens: clarity, outline of leaf

But now the stark dignity of
entrance—Still, the profound change
has come upon them: rooted, they
grip down and begin to awaken

The Pot of Flowers

Pink confused with white
flowers and flowers reversed
take and spill the shaded flame
darting it back
into the lamp's horn

petals aslant darkened with mauve

red where in whorls
petal lays its glow upon petal
round flamegreen throats

petals radiant with transpiercing light
contending
        above
the leaves
reaching up their modest green
from the pot's rim

and there, wholly dark, the pot
gay with rough moss.

To a Dead Journalist

Behind that white brow
now the mind simply sleeps—
the eyes, closed, the
lips, the mouth,

the chin, no longer useful,
the prow of the nose.
But rumors of the news,
unrealizable,

cling still among those
silent, butted features, a
sort of wonder at
this scoop

come now, too late:
beneath the lucid ripples
to have found so monstrous
an obscurity.

MINA LOY   (c. 1883-1966)

Apology of Genius

Ostracized as we are with God—
> The watchers of the civilized wastes
> reverse their signals on our track

> Lepers of the moon
> all magically diseased
> we come among you
> innocent
> of our luminous sores

> unknowing
> how perturbing lights
> our spirit
> on the passion of Man
> until you turn on us your smooth fools' faces
> like buttocks bared in aboriginal mockeries

> We are the sacerdotal clowns
> who feed upon the wind and stars
> and pulverous pastures of poverty

> Our wills are formed
> by curious disciplines
> beyond your laws

> You may give birth to us
> or marry us
> the chances of your flesh
> are not our destiny

> The cuirass of the soul
> still shines
> And we are unaware
> if you confuse
> such brief
> corrosion with possession

In the raw caverns of the Increate
we forge the dusk of Chaos
to that imperious jewelry of the Universe
—the Beautiful

While to your eyes
A delicate crop
of criminal mystic immortelles
stands to the censor's scythe.

Der Blinde Junge

The dam Bellona
littered
her eyeless offspring
Kriegsopfer
upon the pavements of Vienna

Sparkling precipitate
the spectral day
involves
the visionless obstacle

this slow blind face
pushing
its virginal nonentity
against the light

Pure purposeless eremite
of centripetal sentience

Upon the carnose horologe of the ego
the vibrant tendon index moves not

since the black lightning desecrated
the retinal altar

Void and extinct
this planet of the soul
strains from the craving throat
in static flight upslanting

A downy youth's snout
nozzling the sun
drowned in dumfounded instinct

Listen!
illuminati of the coloured earth
How this expressionless "thing"
blows out damnation and concussive dark

Upon a mouth-organ

ELIZABETH DARYUSH   (c. 1891-   )

O strong to bless

O strong to bless
   human misery,
sweet lovingkindness
   comfort thou me;

thou who alone
   mortal hurt canst heal,
most merciful one
   to thee I kneel.

Though man may set
   his soul to harsh ill,
despising thee, yet
   thou lovest still:

yea, though he spurn
   thee, leave thee, yet thou
patient, his return
   awaitest—now

to us, heart-sore,
   solace give; now we,
Mother, yet once more
   come home to thee.

November

Faithless familiars,
　　summer-friends untrue,
once-dear beguilers,
　　now wave ye adieu:

swift warmth and beauty
　　who awhile had won
my glad company,
　　I see you pass on.

Now the still hearth-fire
　　intently gloweth,
now weary desire
　　her dwelling knoweth,

now a newly lit
　　lamp afar shall burn,
the roving spirit
　　stay her and return.

Frustration

God granted, God denies—
　　So faith has said;
But fonder faith still cries
　　Uncomforted.

Now are thy labors o'er—
　　But hope says: 'These
That make me, love I more
　　Than barren ease.'

*Still shalt thou glorify
　　Thy God—*Nay still
Bends desire but to *my*
　　Creating will.

Eyes that queenly sit

Eyes that queenly sit
  At their casement wide,
Mouth that holdeth it
  As a sentry tried,

For the rest, the face
  Howso built it be,
'Tis the fair palace
  Of fair majesty.

Be the friendly house
  Castle high or cot,
Mean or sumptuous,
  Spirit careth not,

If but strength shall show
  At the guarded gate;
If but the window
  Love illuminate.

Fresh Spring

Fresh Spring, in whose deep woods I sought,
  As in your cool abodes I played,
The phantoms of my childish thought,
  The spirits of the faery shade;

Warm Summer, in whose fields I met
  My fancy's every fond device,
Where small imagination set
  The very scenes of Paradise;

Now are your forests high the hall
  Of shades more surely fugitive;
Now raptures lost beyond recall
  In your unsunned recesses live;

Now to your cloudless meadows come
  Forms lit with longing's fiercest flame;
Now truly are your haunts their home
  Eternal, whom with tears I name.

Farewell for a while

Farewell for a while,
  My lov'd one, only;
For earth's little mile
  Of pathway lonely;

For one weary march
  Of sense's pining,
Driv'n out from the arch
  Of joy's enshrining;

For one journey short
  Of thought's sore bearing,
Expelled from the fort
  Of sorrow's sharing;

Till once more the height
  Of truth attainéd,
I'll see the lost light
  Of love unwanéd,

Where (so longing saith)
  Life's road shall leave me—
No more, mortal death,
  Shalt thou deceive me.

(For M.M.B., April 1932)

Autumn, dark wanderer

Autumn, dark wanderer halted here once more,
Grave roamer camped again in our light wood,
With garments ragg'd, but rich and gorgeous-hued,
With the same fraying splendours as before—
Autumn, wan soothsayer, worn gipsy wise,
With melancholy look, but bearing bold,
With lean hard limbs careless of warmth or cold,
With dusky face, and gloomed defiant eyes,

You glanced at summer, and she hung her head;
You gazed, and her fresh cheek with fever burned;
You sighed, and from her flowery vales she turned;
You whispered, and from her fond home she fled:

Now seated by your tattered tent she broods
On timeless heights, eternal solitudes.

Still-Life

Through the open French window the warm sun
lights up the polished breakfast-table, laid
round a bowl of crimson roses, for one—
a service of Worcester porcelain, arrayed
near it a melon, peaches, figs, small hot
rolls in a napkin, fairy rack of toast,
butter in ice, high silver coffee-pot,
and, heaped on a salver, the morning's post.

She comes over the lawn, the young heiress,
from her early walk in her garden-wood,
feeling that life's a table set to bless
her delicate desires with all that's good,

that even the unopened future lies
like a love-letter, full of sweet surprise.

LOUISE BOGAN   (1897-   )
American

Simple Autumnal

The measured blood beats out the year's delay.
The tearless eyes and heart, forbidden grief,
Watch the burned, restless, but abiding leaf,
The brighter branches arming the bright day.

The cone, the curving fruit should fall away,
The vine stem crumble, ripe grain know its sheaf.
Bonded to time, fires should have done, be brief,
But, serfs to sleep, they glitter and they stay.

Because not last nor first, grief in its prime
Wakes in the day, and hears of life's intent.
Sorrow would break the seal stamped over time
And set the baskets where the bough is bent.

Full season's come, yet filled trees keep the sky
And never scent the ground where they must lie.

Henceforth, From the Mind

Henceforth, from the mind,
For your whole joy, must spring
Such joy as you may find
In any earthly thing,
And every time and place
Will take your thought for grace.

Henceforth, from the tongue,
From shallow speech alone,
Comes joy you thought, when young,
Would wring you to the bone,
Would pierce you to the heart
And spoil its stop and start.

Henceforward, from the shell,
Wherein you heard, and wondered
At oceans like a bell
So far from ocean sundered—
A smothered sound that sleeps
Long lost within lost deeps,

Will chime you change and hours,
The shadow of increase,
Will sound you flowers
Born under troubled peace—
Henceforth, henceforth
Will echo sea and earth.

Exhortation

Give over seeking bastard joy
Nor cast for fortune's side-long look.
Indifference can be your toy;
The bitter heart can be your book.
(Its lesson torment never shook.)

In the cold heart, as on a page,
Spell out the gentle syllable
That puts short limit to your rage
And curdles the straight fire of hell,
Compassing all, so all is well.

Read how, though passion sets in storm
And grief's a comfort, and the young
Touch at the flint when it is warm,
It is the dead we live among,
The dead given motion, and a tongue.

The dead, long trained to cruel sport
And the crude gossip of the grave;
The dead, who pass in motley sort,
Whom sun nor sufferance can save.
Face them. They sneer. Do not be brave.

Know once for all: their snare is set
Even now; be sure their trap is laid;
And you will see your lifetime yet
Come to their terms, your plans unmade,—
And be belied, and be betrayed.

JANET LEWIS   (1899-   )
American

Girl Help

Mild and slow and young,
She moves about the room,
And stirs the summer dust
With her wide broom.

In the warm, lofted air,
Soft lips together pressed,
Soft wispy hair,
She stops to rest,

And stops to breathe,
Amid the summer hum,
The great white lilac bloom
Scented with days to come.

Love Poem

Instinctively, unwittingly,
I came unto your hand,
For it dispenses quietness
With graciousness as grand

As the daughter of Demeter
In shadowy croft or glen
Dispensing sleep eternal
To tired working men.

The harvester lays down his scythe;
And lays his basket down
The vintner, and his heavy head
In vineyards overgrown.

For Elizabeth Madox Roberts
  Who died March 13, 1941

From the confusion of estranging years,
The imperfections of the changing heart,
This hour leaves only tears;
Tears, and my earliest love, Elizabeth, and changeless art.

In the Egyptian Museum

Under the lucent glass,
Closed from the living air,
Clear in electric glare
That does not change nor pass,
Armlet and amulet
And woven gold are laid
Beside the turquoise braid
With coral flowers inset.

The beetle, lapis, green,
Graved with the old device,
And linen brown with spice,
Long centuries unseen,
And this most gracious wreath,
Exiled from the warm hair,
Meet now the curious stare—
All talismans of death.

All that the anguished mind
Most nobly could invent,
To one devotion bent,
That death seem less unkind;
That the degraded flesh,
Grown spiritless and cold,
Be housed in beaten gold,
A rich and rigid mesh.

Such pain is garnered here
In every close-locked case,
Concentrate in this place
Year after fading year,
That, while I wait, a cry,
As from beneath the glass,
Pierces me with "Alas
That the beloved must die!"

Lines with a Gift of Herbs

The summer's residue
In aromatic leaf,
Shrunken and dry, yet true
In fragrance, their belief,

These from the hard earth drew
Essence of rosemary,
Lavender, faintly blue,
While unconfused nearby

From the same earth distilled
Grey sage and savory,
Each one distinctly willed,—
Stoic morality.

The Emperor said, "Though all
Conspire to break thy will,
Clear stone, thou emerald, shall
Be ever emerald still."

And these, small, unobserved,
Through summer chemistry,
Have all their might conserved
In treasure, finally.

Helen Grown Old

We have forgotten Paris, and his fate.
We have not much inquired
If Menelaus from the Trojan gate
Returning found the long desired
Immortal beauty by his hearth. Then late,

Late, long past the morning hour,
Could even she recapture from the dawn
The young delightful love? When the dread power
That forced her will was gone,
When fell the last charred tower,

When the last flame had faded from the cloud,
And by the darkening sea
The plain lay empty of the arméd crowd,
Then was she free
Who had been ruled by passion blind and proud?

Then did she find with him whom first she chose
Before the desperate flight,
At last, repose
In love still radiant at the edge of night,
As fair as in the morning? No one knows.

No one has cared to say. The story clings
To the tempestuous years, by passion bound,
Like Helen. No one brings
A tale of quiet love. The fading sound
Is blent of falling embers, weeping kings.

YVOR WINTERS   (1900-1968)
American

Quod Tegit Omnia

Earth darkens and is beaded
with a sweat of bushes and
the bear comes forth;
the mind, stored with
magnificence, proceeds into
the mystery of time, now
certain of its choice of
passion, but uncertain of the
passion's end.

        When
Plato temporizes on the nature
of the plumage of the soul the
wind hums in the feathers as
across a cord impeccable in
tautness but of no mind:

        Time,
the sine-pondere, most
imperturbable of elements,
assumes its own proportions
silently, of its own properties—
an excellence at which one
sighs.

        Adventurer in
living fact, the poet
mounts into the spring,
upon his tongue the taste of
air becoming body: is
embedded in this crystalline
precipitate of time.

The Slow Pacific Swell

Far out of sight forever stands the sea,
Bounding the land with pale tranquillity.
When a small child, I watched it from a hill
At thirty miles or more. The vision still
Lies in the eye, soft blue and far away:
The rain has washed the dust from April day;
Paint-brush and lupine lie against the ground;
The wind above the hill-top has the sound
Of distant water in unbroken sky;
Dark and precise the little steamers ply—
Firm in direction they seem not to stir.
That is illusion. The artificer
Of quiet, distance holds me in a vise
And holds the ocean steady to my eyes.

Once when I rounded Flattery, the sea
Hove its loose weight like sand to tangle me
Upon the washing deck, to crush the hull;
Subsiding, dragged flesh at the bone. The skull
Felt the retreating wash of dreaming hair.
Half drenched in dissolution, I lay bare.
I scarcely pulled myself erect; I came
Back slowly, slowly knew myself the same.
That was the ocean. From the ship we saw
Gray whales for miles: the long sweep of the jaw,
The blunt head plunging clean above the wave.
And one rose in a tent of sea and gave
A darkening shudder; water fell away;
The whale stood shining, and then sank in spray.

A landsman, I. The sea is but a sound.
I would be near it on a sandy mound,
And hear the steady rushing of the deep
While I lay stinging in the sand with sleep.
I have lived inland long. The land is numb.
It stands beneath the feet, and one may come
Walking securely, till the sea extends
Its limber margin, and precision ends.
By night a chaos of commingling power,
The whole Pacific hovers hour by hour.
The slow Pacific swell stirs on the sand,
Sleeping to sink away, withdrawing land,
Heaving and wrinkled in the moon, and blind;
Or gathers seaward, ebbing out of mind.

The Marriage

Incarnate for our marriage you appeared,
Flesh living in the spirit and endeared
By minor graces and slow sensual change.
Through every nerve we made our spirits range.
We fed our minds on every mortal thing:
The lacy fronds of carrots in the spring,
Their flesh sweet on the tongue, the salty wine
From bitter grapes, which gathered through the vine
The mineral drouth of autumn concentrate,
Wild spring in dream escaping, the debate
Of flesh and spirit on those vernal nights,
Its resolution in naive delights,
The young kids bleating softly in the rain—
All this to pass, not to return again.
And when I found your flesh did not resist,
It was the living spirit that I kissed,
It was the spirit's change in which I lay:
Thus, mind in mind we waited for the day.
When flesh shall fall away, and, falling, stand
Wrinkling with shadow over face and hand,
Still I shall meet you on the verge of dust
And know you as a faithful vestige must.
And, in commemoration of our lust,
May our heirs seal us in a single urn,
A single spirit never to return.

On a View of Pasadena from the Hills

From the high terrace porch I watch the dawn.
No light appears, though dark has mostly gone,
Sunk from the cold and monstrous stone. The hills
Lie naked but not light. The darkness spills
Down the remoter gulleys; pooled, will stay
Too low to melt, not yet alive with day.
Below the windows, the lawn, matted deep
Under its close-cropped tips with dewy sleep,
Gives off a faint hush, all its plushy swarm
Alive with coolness reaching to be warm.
Gray windows at my back, the massy frame
Dull with the blackness that has not a name;
But down below, the garden is still young,
Of five years' growth, perhaps, and terrace-hung,
Drop by slow drop of seeping concrete walls.
Such are the bastions of our pastorals!

Here are no palms! They once lined country ways,
Where old white houses glared down dusty days,
With small round towers, blunt-headed through small trees.
Those towers are now the hiving place of bees.
The palms were coarse; their leaves hung thick with dust;
The roads were muffled deep. But now deep rust
Has fastened on the wheels that labored then.
Peace to all such, and to all sleeping men!
I lived my childhood there, a passive dream
In the expanse of that recessive scheme.

Slow air, slow fire! O deep delay of Time!
That summer crater smoked like slaking lime,
The hills so dry, so dense the underbrush,
That where I pushed my way the giant hush
Was changed to soft explosion as the sage
Broke down to powdered ash, the sift of age,
And fell along my path, a shadowy rift.

On these rocks now no burning ashes drift;
Mowed lawn has crept along the granite bench;
The yellow blossoms of acacia drench
The dawn with pollen; and, with waxen green,
The long leaves of the eucalypti screen
The closer hills from view—lithe, tall, and fine,
And nobly clad with youth, they bend and shine.
The small dark pool, jutting with living rock,
Trembles at every atmospheric shock,
Blurred to its depth with the cold living ooze.
From cloudy caves, heavy with summer dews,
The shyest and most tremulous beings stir,
The pulsing of their fins a lucent blur,
That, like illusion, glances off the view.
The pulsing mouths, like metronomes, are true.

This is my father's house, no homestead here
That I shall live in, but a shining sphere
Of glass and glassy moments, frail surprise,
My father's phantasy of Paradise;
Which melts upon his death, which he attained
With loss of heart for every step he gained.
Too firmly gentle to displace the great,
He crystallized this vision somewhat late;
Forbidden now to climb the garden stair,
He views the terrace from a window chair.
His friends, hard shaken by some twenty years,
Tremble with palsy and with senile fears,
In their late middle age gone cold and gray.
Fine men, now broken. That the vision stay,
They spend astutely their depleted breath,
With tired ironic faces wait for death.

Below the garden the hills fold away.
Deep in the valley, a mist fine as spray,
Ready to shatter into spinning light,
Conceals the city at the edge of night.
The city, on the tremendous valley floor,
Draws its dream deeper for an instant more,
Superb on solid loam, and breathing deep,
Poised for a moment at the edge of sleep.

Cement roads mark the hills, wide, bending tree
Of cliff and headland. Dropping toward the sea,
Through suburb after suburb, vast ravines
Swell to the summer drone of fine machines.
The driver, melting down the distance here,
May cast in flight the faint hoof of a deer
Or pass the faint head set perplexedly.
And man-made stone outgrows the living tree,
And at its rising, air is shaken, men
Are shattered, and the tremor swells again,
Extending to the naked salty shore,
Rank with the sea, which crumbles evermore.

Before Disaster
Winter, 1932-33

Evening traffic homeward burns,
Swift and even on the turns,
Drifting weight in triple rows,
Fixed relation and repose.
This one edges out and by,
Inch by inch with steady eye.
But should error be increased,
Mass and moment are released;
Matter loosens, flooding blind,
Levels drivers to its kind.
   Ranks of nations thus descend,
Watchful to a stormy end.
By a moment's calm beguiled,
I have got a wife and child.
Fool and scoundrel guide the State.
Peace is whore to Greed and Hate.
Nowhere may I turn to flee:
Action is security.
Treading change with savage heel,
We must live or die by steel.

Heracles*
for Don Stanford

Eurystheus, trembling, called me to the throne,
Alcmena's son, heavy with thews and still.
He drove me on my fatal road alone:
I went, subservient to Hera's will.

For, when I had resisted, she had struck
Out of the sky and spun my wit: I slew
My children, quicker than a stroke of luck,
With motion lighter than my sinews knew.

Compelled down ways obscure with analogue
To force the Symbols of the Zodiac—
Bright Lion, Boundless Hydra, Fiery Dog—
I spread them on my arms as on a rack:

Spread them and broke them in the groaning wood,
And yet the Centaur stung me from afar,
His blood envenomed with the Hydra's blood:
Thence was I outcast from the earthy war.

Nessus the Centaur, with his wineskin full,
His branch and thyrsus, and his fleshy grip—
Her whom he could not force he yet could gull.
And she drank poison from his bearded lip.

Older than man, evil with age, is life:
Injustice, direst perfidy, my bane
Drove me to win my lover and my wife;
By love and justice I at last was slain.

The numbered Beings of the wheeling track
I carried singly to the empty throne,
And yet, when I had come exhausted back,
Was forced to wait without the gate alone.

Commanded thus to pause before the gate,
I felt from my hot breast the tremors pass,
White flame dissecting the corrupted State,
Eurystheus vibrant in his den of brass:

Vibrant with horror, though a jewelled king,
Lest the heat mounting, madness turn my brain
For one dry moment, and the palace ring
With crystal terror ere I turn again.

This stayed me, too: my life was not my own,
But I my life's; a god I was, not man.
Grown Absolute, I slew my flesh and bone;
Timeless, I knew the Zodiac my span.

This was my grief, that out of grief I grew—
Translated as I was from earth at last,
From the sad pain that Deianira knew.
Transmuted slowly in a fiery blast,

Perfect, and moving perfectly, I raid
Eternal silence to eternal ends:
And Deianira, an imperfect shade,
Retreats in silence as my arc descends.

---

*Heracles is treated as a Sun-god, the particular statement used being that of Anthon's *Classical Dictionary*. Allegorically, he is the artist, in hand-to-hand or semi-intuitive combat with experience. [author's note]

John Sutter

I was the patriarch of the shining land,
Of the blond summer and metallic grain;
Men vanished at the motion of my hand,
And when I beckoned they would come again.

The earth grew dense with grain at my desire;
The shade was deepened at the springs and streams;
Moving in dust that clung like pillared fire,
The gathering herds grew heavy in my dreams.

Across the mountains, naked from the heights,
Down to the valley broken settlers came,
And in my houses feasted through the nights,
Rebuilt their sinews and assumed a name.

In my clear rivers my own men discerned
The motive for the ruin and the crime—
Gold heavier than earth, a wealth unearned,
Loot, for two decades, from the heart of Time.

Metal, intrinsic value, deep and dense,
Preanimate, inimitable, still,
Real, but an evil with no human sense,
Dispersed the mind to concentrate the will.

Grained by alchemic change, the human kind
Turned from themselves to rivers and to rocks;
With dynamite broke metal unrefined;
Measured their moods by geologic shocks.

With knives they dug the metal out of stone;
Turned rivers back, for gold through ages piled,
Drove knives to hearts, and faced the gold alone;
Valley and river ruined and reviled;

Reviled and ruined me, my servant slew,
Strangled him from the figtree by my door.
When they had done what fury bade them do,
I was a cursing beggar, stripped and sore.

What end impersonal, what breathless age,
Incontinent of quiet and of years,
What calm catastrophe will yet assuage
This final drouth of penitential tears?

Sir Gawaine and the Green Knight

Reptilian green the wrinkled throat,
Green as a bough of yew the beard;
He bent his head, and so I smote;
Then for a thought my vision cleared.

The head dropped clean; he rose and walked;
He fixed his fingers in the hair;
The head was unabashed and talked;
I understood what I must dare.

His flesh, cut down, arose and grew.
He bade me wait the season's round,
And then, when he had strength anew,
To meet him on his native ground.

The year declined; and in his keep
I passed in joy a thriving yule;
And whether waking or in sleep,
I lived in riot like a fool.

He beat the woods to bring me meat.
His lady, like a forest vine,
Grew in my arms; the growth was sweet;
And yet what thoughtless force was mine!

By practice and conviction formed,
With ancient stubbornness ingrained,
Although her body clung and swarmed,
My own identity remained.

Her beauty, lithe, unholy, pure,
Took shapes that I had never known;
And had I once been insecure,
Had grafted laurel in my bone.

And then, since I had kept the trust,
Had loved the lady, yet was true,
The knight withheld his giant thrust
And let me go with what I knew.

I left the green bark and the shade,
Where growth was rapid, thick, and still;
I found a road that men had made
And rested on a drying hill.

Time and the Garden

The spring has darkened with activity.
The future gathers in vine, bush, and tree:
Persimmon, walnut, loquat, fig, and grape,
Degrees and kinds of color, taste, and shape.
These will advance in their due series, space
The season like a tranquil dwelling-place.
And yet excitement swells me, vein by vein:
I long to crowd the little garden, gain
Its sweetness in my hand and crush it small
And taste it in a moment, time and all!
These trees, whose slow growth measures off my years,
I would expand to greatness. No one hears,
And I am still retarded in duress!
And this is like that other restlessness
To seize the greatness not yet fairly earned,
One which the tougher poets have discerned—
Gascoigne, Ben Jonson, Greville, Raleigh, Donne,
Poets who wrote great poems, one by one,
And spaced by many years, each line an act
Through which few labor, which no men retract.
This passion is the scholar's heritage,
The imposition of a busy age,
The passion to condense from book to book
Unbroken wisdom in a single look,
Though we know well that when this fix the head,
The mind's immortal, but the man is dead.

A Summer Commentary

When I was young, with sharper sense,
The farthest insect cry I heard
Could stay me; through the trees, intense,
I watched the hunter and the bird.

Where is the meaning that I found?
Or was it but a state of mind,
Some old penumbra of the ground,
In which to be but not to find?

Now summer grasses, brown with heat,
Have crowded sweetness through the air;
The very roadside dust is sweet;
Even the unshadowed earth is fair.

The soft voice of the nesting dove,
And the dove in soft erratic flight
Like a rapid hand within a glove,
Caress the silence and the light.

Amid the rubble, the fallen fruit,
Fermenting in its rich decay,
Smears brandy on the trampling boot
And sends it sweeter on its way.

To the Holy Spirit
>   from a deserted graveyard
>   in the Salinas Valley

Immeasurable haze:
The desert valley spreads
Up golden river-beds
As if in other days.
Trees rise and thin away,
And past the trees, the hills,
Pure line and shade of dust,
Bear witness to our wills:
We see them, for we must;
Calm in deceit, they stay.

High noon returns the mind
Upon its local fact:
Dry grass and sand; we find
No vision to distract.
Low in the summer heat,
Naming old graves, are stones
Pushed here and there, the seat
Of nothing, and the bones
Beneath are similar:
Relics of lonely men,
Brutal and aimless, then,
As now, irregular.

These are thy fallen sons,
Thou whom I try to reach.
Thou whom the quick eye shuns,
Thou dost elude my speech.
Yet when I go from sense
And trace thee down in thought,
I meet thee, then, intense,
And know thee as I ought.
But thou art mind alone,
And I, alas, am bound
Pure mind to flesh and bone,
And flesh and bone to ground.

These had no thought: at most
Dark faith and blinding earth.
Where is the trammeled ghost?
Was there another birth?
Only one certainty
Beside thine unfleshed eye,
Beside the spectral tree,
Can I discern: these die.
All of this stir of age,
Though it elude my sense
Into what heritage
I know not, seems to fall,
Quiet beyond recall,
Into irrelevance.

At the San Francisco Airport

To my daughter, 1954

This is the terminal: the light
Gives perfect vision, false and hard;
The metal glitters, deep and bright.
Great planes are waiting in the yard—
They are already in the night.

And you are here beside me, small,
Contained and fragile, and intent
On things that I but half recall—
Yet going whither you are bent.
I am the past, and that is all.

But you and I in part are one:
The frightened brain, the nervous will,
The knowledge of what must be done,
The passion to acquire the skill
To face that which you dare not shun.

The rain of matter upon sense
Destroys me momently. The score:
There comes what will come. The expense
Is what one thought, and something more—
One's being and intelligence.

This is the terminal, the break.
Beyond this point, on lines of air,
You take the way that you must take;
And I remain in light and stare—
In light, and nothing else, awake.

J. V. CUNNINGHAM   (1911-   )
American

Epigraph from *The Judge Is Fury*

These the assizes: here the charge, denial,
Proof and disproof: the poem is the trial.
Experience is defendant, and the jury
Peers of tradition, and the judge is fury.

Lector Aere Perennior

Poets survive in fame.
But how can substance trade
The body for a name
Wherewith no soul's arrayed?

No form inspires the clay
Now breathless of what was
Save the imputed sway
Of some Pythagoras,

Some man so deftly mad
His metamorphosed shade,
Leaving the flesh it had,
Breathes on the words they made.

The Phoenix

More than the ash stays you from nothingness!
Nor here nor there is a consuming pyre!
Your essence is in infinite regress
That burns with varying consistent fire,
Mythical bird that bears in burying!

I have not found you in exhausted breath
That carves its image on the Northern air,
I have not found you on the glass of death
Though I am told that I shall find you there,
Imperturbable in the final cold,

There where the North wind shapes white cenotaphs,
There where snowdrifts cover the fathers' mound,
Unmarked but for these wintry epitaphs,
Still are you singing there without sound,
Your mute voice on the crystal embers flinging.

Ars Amoris

Speak to her heart!
That manic force
When wits depart
Forbids remorse.

Dream with her dreaming
Until her lust
Seems to her seeming
An act of trust!

Do without doing!
Love's wilful potion
Veils the ensuing,
And brief, commotion.

Agnosco Veteris Vestigia Flammae

I have been here. Dispersed in meditation,
I sense the traces of the old surmise—
Passion dense as fatigue, faithful as pain,
As joy foreboding. O my void, my being
In the suspended sources of experience,
Massive in promise, unhistorical
Being of unbeing, of all futures full,
Unrealised in none, how love betrays you,
Turns you to process and a fluid fact
Whose future specifies its past, whose past
Precedes it, and whose history is its being.

Meditation on Statistical Method

Plato, despair!
We prove by norms
How numbers bear
Empiric forms,

How random wrong
Will average right
If time be long
And error slight,

But in our hearts
Hyperbole
Curves and departs
To infinity.

Error is boundless.
Nor hope nor doubt,
Though both be groundless,
Will average out.

Meditation on a Memoir

Who knows his will?
Who knows what mood
His hours fulfil?
His griefs conclude?

Surf of illusion
Spins from the deep
And skilled delusion
Sustains his sleep.

When silence hears
In its delight
The tide of tears
In the salt night,

And stirs, and tenses,
Who knows what themes,
What lunar senses,
Compel his dreams?

To the Reader

Time will assuage.
Time's verses bury
Margin and page
In commentary,

For gloss demands
A gloss annexed
Till busy hands
Blot out the text,

And all's coherent.
Search in this gloss
No text inherent:
The text was loss.

The gain is gloss.

from *Epigrams: A Journal*

8.

If wisdom, as it seems it is,
Be the recovery of some bliss
From the conditions of disaster—
Terror the servant, man the master—
It does not follow we should seek
Crises to prove ourselves unweak.
Much of our lives, God knows, is error,
But who will trifle with unrest?
These fools who would solicit terror,
Obsessed with being unobsessed,
Professionals of experience
Who have disasters to withstand them
As if fear never had unmanned them,
Flaunt a presumptuous innocence.

I have preferred indifference.

23.

Dark thoughts are my companions. I have wined
With lewdness and with crudeness, and I find
Love is my enemy, dispassionate hate
Is my redemption though it come too late—
Though I come to it with a broken head
In the cat-house of the dishevelled dead.

27.   *On the Calculus*

From almost naught to almost all I flee,
And *almost* has almost confounded me,
Zero my limit, and infinity.

35.

Hang up your weaponed wit
Who were destroyed by it.
If silence fails, then grace
Your speech with commonplace
And studiously amaze
Your audience with his phrase.
He will commend your wit
When you abandon it.

42.   With a copy of Swift's Works

Underneath this pretty cover
Lies Vanessa's, Stella's lover.
You that undertake this story
For his life nor death be sorry
Who the Absolute so loved
Motion to its zero moved,
Till immobile in that chill
Fury hardened in the will,
And the trival, bestial flesh
In its jacket ceased to thresh,
And the soul none dare forgive
Quiet lay, and ceased to live.

43.

In whose will is our peace? Thou happiness,
Thou ghostly promise, to thee I confess
Neither in thine nor love's nor in that form
Disquiet hints at have I yet been warm;
And if I rest not till I rest in thee
Cold as thy grace, whose hand shall comfort me?

from *Doctor Drink*

8.

On a cold night I came through the cold rain
And false snow to the wind shrill on your pane
With no hope and no anger and no fear:
Who are you? and with whom do you sleep here?

from *Trivial, Vulgar, and Exalted*

19.

I had gone broke, and got set to come back,
And lost, on a hot day and a fast track,
On a long shot at long odds, a black mare
By Hatred out of Envy by Despair.

EDGAR BOWERS   (1924-   )
American

The Stoic: for Laura von Courten

All winter long you listened for the boom
Of distant cannon wheeled into their place.
Sometimes outside beneath a bombers' moon
You stood alone to watch the searchlights trace

Their careful webs against the boding sky,
While miles away on Munich's vacant square
The bombs lunged down with an unruly cry
Whose blast you saw yet could but faintly hear.

And might have turned your eyes upon the gleam
Of a thousand years of snow, where near the clouds
The Alps ride massive to their full extreme,
And season after season glacier crowds

The dark, persistent smudge of conifers.
Or seen beyond the hedge and through the trees
The shadowy forms of cattle on the furze,
Their dim coats white with mist against the freeze.

Or thought instead of other times than these,
Of other countries and of other sights:
Eternal Venice sinking by degrees
Into the very water that she lights;

Reflected in canals, the lucid dome
Of Maria dell' Salute at your feet,
Her triple spires disfigured by the foam.
Remembered in Berlin the parks, the neat

Footpaths and lawns, the clean spring foliage,
Where just short weeks before, a bomb, unaimed,
Released a frightened lion from its cage,
Which in the mottled dark that trees enflamed

Killed one who hurried homeward from the raid.
And by yourself there standing in the chill
You must, with so much known, have been afraid
And chosen such a mind of constant will,

Which, though all time corrode with constant hurt,
Remains, until it occupies no space,
That which it is; and passionless, inert,
Becomes at last no meaning and no place.

Dark Earth and Summer

Earth is dark where you rest
Though a little winter grass
Glistens in icy furrows.
There, cautious, as I pass,

Squirrels run, leaving stains
Of their nervous, minute feet
Over the tombs; and near them
Birds grey and gravely sweet.

I have come, warm of breath,
To sustain unbodied cold,
Removed from life and seeking
Darkness where flesh is old,

Flesh old and summer waxing,
Quick eye in the sunny lime,
Sweet apricots in silence
Falling—precious in time,

All radiant as a voice, deep
As their oblivion. Only as I may,
I come, remember, wait,
Ignorant in grief, yet stay.

What you are will outlast
The warm variety of risk,
Caught in the wide, implacable,
Clear gaze of the basilisk.

The Virgin Mary

The hovering and huge, dark, formless sway
That nature moves by laws we contemplate
We name for lack of name as order, fate,
God, principle, or primum mobile.
But in that graven image, word made wood
By skillful faith of him to whom she was
Eternal nature, first and final cause,
The form of knowledge knowledge understood
Bound human thought against the dark we find.
And body took the image of the mind
To shape in chaos a congruent form
Of will and matter, equal, side by side,
Upon the act of faith, within the norm
Of carnal being, blind and glorified.

From William Tyndale to John Frith*

The letters I, your lone friend, write in sorrow
Will not contain my sorrow: it is mine,
Not yours who stand for burning in my place.
Be certain of your fate. Though some, benign,
Will urge by their sweet threats malicious love
And counsel dangerous fear of violence,
Theirs is illusion's goodness proving fair—
Against your wisdom—worldly innocence
And just persuasions' old hypocrisy.
Making their choice, reflect what you become:
Horror and misery bringing ruin where
The saintly mind has treacherously gone numb;
Despair in the deceit of your remorse
As, doubly heretic, you waste your past
Recanting, by all pitied, honorless,
Until you choose more easy death at last.
Think too of me. Sometimes in morning dark
I let my candle gutter and sit here
Brooding, as shadows fill my cell and sky
Breaks pale outside my window; then the dear
Companionship we spent working for love
Compels me to achieve a double portion.
In spite of age, insanity, despair,
Grief, or declining powers, we have done
What passes to the living of all men
Beyond our weariness. The fire shall find
Me hidden here, although its pain be less
If you have gone to it with half my mind,
Leaving me still enough to fasten flesh
Against the stake, flesh absolute with will.
And should your human powers and my need
Tremble at last and grow faint, worn, and ill,
Pain be too much to think of, fear destroy,
And animal reluctance from the womb,
Endurance of your end's integrity,
Be strong in this: heaven shall be your tomb.

---

*John Frith, Tyndale's most loyal disciple, returned to England from the
continent in 1533, when he was thirty years old. He was arrested and
burned at the stake. This letter would have been written to Frith in
prison from Tyndale in Holland, where, not long after, he too was
imprisoned and burned at the stake for heresy. [author's note]

Adam's Song to Heaven

You shall be as gods, knowing good and evil

O depth sufficient to desire,
Ghostly abyss wherein perfection hides,
    Purest effect and cause, you are
The mirror and the image love provides.

All else is waste, though you reveal
Lightly upon your luminous bent shore
    Color, shape, odor, weight, and voice,
Bright mocking hints that were not there before,

And all your progeny time holds
In timeless birth and death. But, when, for bliss,
    Loneliness would possess its like,
Mine is the visage yours leans down to kiss.

Beautiful you are, fair deceit!
Knowledge is joy where your unseeing eyes
    Shine with the tears that I have wept
To be the sum of all your thoughts devise.

Flawless you are, unlimited
By other than yourself, yet suffer pain
    Of the nostalgias I have felt
For love beyond the end your eyes contain;

Then, solitary, drift, inert,
Through the abyss where you would have me go
    And, lost to your desire at last,
Ravish the waste for what you cannot know.

What are you then! Delirium
Receives the image I despair to keep,
    And knowledge in your somber depth
Embraces your perfection and your sleep.

The Astronomers of Mont Blanc

Who are you there that, from your icy tower,
Explore the colder distances, the far
Escape of your whole universe to night;
That watch the moon's blue craters, shadowy crust,
And blunted mountains mildly drift and glare,
Ballooned in ghostly earnest on your sight;
Who are you, and what hope persuades your trust?

It is your hope that you will know the end
And compass of our ignorant restraint
There in lost time, where what was done is done
Forever as a havoc overhead.
Aging, you search to master in the faint
Persistent fortune which you gaze upon
The perfect order trusted to the dead.

The Mirror

Father, I loved you as a child, and still,
When trouble bruises him whom I retrace
Back to the time I cannot know, I fill,
By my desire, the possible with grace,
And wait your coming. Then I see my face,
Breathed by some other presence on the chill
Illumination of this mortal glass,
Gleam from the dark to struggle in your will.

In that fixed place, around me, others move,
Vivid with long conclusion, who, once dead,
Quickened the little moment I could prove;
And, though I seem to live, there, at my head,
As if the thought translating all I see,
He stands, who was my future, claiming me.

CATHERINE DAVIS   (1924-   )
American

Insights

1.   To C. D. M.

And what of you? You also shall not say
What time and time's remorselessness betray.
How can you think your silence is complete?
The heart fails, but the pitiless years repeat
The sure, unspeakable malice of the dead:
The grief you came to was the past you fled.

2.   To the spirit of Baudelaire

Wind of the wing of madness! What is this?
O you that shuddered then, what mantic bird?
What travesty, dark spirit, of the Word?
What last cold exhalation of your bliss?
What passage to what end? Speechless abyss.

3.

Idleness, wretch, you waste in this disease—
Disquiet and excess—this wretched ease!
Look round, look round: these alleycats, this slum!
Mange prowls and ravens blighted Christendom.

4.   In New York

What can I do here? I could learn to lie;
Mouth Freud and Zen; rub shoulders at the "Y"
With this year's happy few; greet every hack—
The rough hyena, the young trimmer pack,
The Village idiot—with an equal eye;
And always scratch the true backscratcher's back.
All this, in second Rome, I'd learn to do;
Hate secretly and climb; get money; quit,
An absolutely stoic hypocrite.
This, but not more. New York is something new:
The toadies like the toads they toady to.

5.

Pity, Catullus, these late revelers
Who celebrate their passing with a shout,
These idle, disabused malingerers
Who wait defeat, as in a barbarous rout
Amid a wreck of cities, empires lost:
They are as faggots in a holocaust.
Pity, among the rest, this sparrow verse.

6.   Hesperides

And must I all die? Herrick, there are tears
Which now not even your *thirty thousand years*,
Nor all your Western Isle, is proof against—
Tears not to be denied, nor countenanced.
For who shall be the guardians of such gold?
The red sun rides the sea: The Nymphs are old.
If we haul anchor, ply the dusky oars
Outward and outward from the burnished shores,
Although the apples hang as now, as fair,
What sound will break the glowing silence there?
But all I know is that I do not know:
Let me write well, not weep, and leave it so.

7.   Guercino's *Et in Arcadia ego*

Even in Arcady, the mouse, the fly,
And Death agape confront the passersby.

ALAN STEPHENS (1925-   )
American

Prologue: Moments in a Glade

Abiding snake:
            At thirty-four
By unset spirit driven here
I watch the season. Warily
My private senses start to alter,
Emerging at no sign from me
In the stone colors of my matter.

You that I met in a dim path,
Exact responder with a wrath
Wise in conditions, long secure,
Settled expertly for the kill
You keep a dull exterior
Over quick fiber holding still . . .

Rocking a little, in a coarse
Glitter beneath fine, vacant space,
The hillside scrub oak interlocked
Where year by year, and unattended,
And by abrasive forcings raked
Against itself, it had ascended.

And yet below me sixty feet
A well of air stood dark and sweet
Over clean boulders and a spring.
And I descended through a ripple
Of upper leaves, till noticing
That a rock pattern had grown supple,

And whirred, I quietly backed off.
I have considered you enough.
The rattle stopped; the rigid coil,
Rustling, began to flow; the head,
Still watching me, swayed down to crawl,
Tilting dead leaves on either side.

You in the adventitious there,
Passion, but passion making sure,
Attending singly what it chose
And so condemned to lie in wait
Stilled in variety—to doze
Or wake as seasons fluctuate,

Eyes open always, the warm prey
At best but happening your way.
And I too slowly found a stone
To break your spine; and I have known
That what I will have surely spoken
Abides thus—may be yet thus broken.

HELEN PINKERTON (1927-   )
American

Indecision

Identity, known or unknown, survives
The lost untempered anguish and the waste.
Its hardness holds, affirming him who grieves.
What he is not and is it says till death.
Then as a diamond when the chisel cleaves
It is a perfect whole or only dust.

Unless against time's claim of absolute,
Spirit should be Christ's flesh—not habitant—
And rest, itself unchanged, in time's estate,
The righteousness of days one may have spent
Learning the surest speech, the oldest act,
Will have but sanctity of precedent.

And while we live we still are free to choose
In his perfected death and resurrection
To see all minor deaths and thereby lose
Delight in change for final absolution.
Or we may wait the death none can refuse
Which will, itself, be in time's disposition.

Error Pursued

Satan in Eden "was constrain'd
Into a beast."
All of the proud, like him, are pained,
And you not least,
To wear the flesh of which we all are made.

It was a means for him and Christ.
Shrewder than we,
Each knew for what he sacrificed.
Carnality
Destroys when not accepted and allayed.

It is the gift of punishment
That you refuse.
You say you sin without consent
And thus excuse
Self-pity and self-hate—and your despair.

For self is faithless to its end.
Not wife or child
Will fail as badly, nor has friend
As soon beguiled.
It is your way, and you are most aware.

CHARLES GULLANS   (1929-   )
American

Autumn Burial: A Meditation

O Mors, Mors quid ages, quove feres pedem?

What business have I here
  At such an hour?
  Each way is fear;
And fear is a persistent power,

Clinging to every breath,
  As cold as love,
  As intimate as death,
Which I cannot remove,

Since fear is my concern
  For what I lose,
  For what is past return,
For what I did not choose

To be my part of terror
  In the long act
  Of life and error—
And nothing that I can retract!

How shall I use the life
  Not mine to use,
  Involved in the old strife
Where feelings but confuse

The issue with the hour;
  Where, tentative,
  The slow mind's power
Seems less than what I need to live?

Knowledge is slow to form;
  And I grow old,
  Seeking, not to be warm
With life, but to be cold,

Almost indifferent,
  Almost unmoved;
  Although intent,
Alert, impartial, and removed.

Even his feeble dust
  Shall strike no fears
  When all, if less than just,
Is just as it appears.

Things are as they must be.
  No one retracts.
  Relentlessly,
We are the issue of our acts.

We are the past, whose past
  Was our creation,
  Where everything at last
Must come to perfect station.

This is the end of tears.
  No more lament.
  Through all the years,
Immutable stands this event.

THOM GUNN   (1929-   )

In Santa Maria Del Popolo

Waiting for when the sun an hour or less
Conveniently oblique makes visible
The painting on one wall of this recess
By Caravaggio, of the Roman School,
I see how shadow in the painting brims
With a real shadow, drowning all shapes out
But a dim horse's haunch and various limbs,
Until the very subject is in doubt.

But evening gives the act, beneath the horse
And one indifferent groom, I see him sprawl,
Foreshortened from the head, with hidden face,
Where he has fallen, Saul becoming Paul.
O wily painter, limiting the scene
From a cacophany of dusty forms
To the one convulsion, what is it you mean
In that wide gesture of the lifting arms?

No Ananias croons a mystery yet,
Casting the pain out under name of sin.
The painter saw what was, an alternate
Candor and secrecy inside the skin.
He painted, elsewhere, that firm insolent
Young whore in Venus' clothes, those pudgy cheats,
Those sharpers; and was strangled, as things went,
For money, by one such picked off the streets.

I turn, hardly enlightened, from the chapel
To the dim interior of the church instead,
In which there kneel already several people,
Mostly old women: each head closeted
In tiny fists holds comfort as it can.
Their poor arms are too tired for more than this
—For the large gesture of solitary man,
Resisting, by embracing, nothingness.

N. SCOTT MOMADAY   (1934-   )
American

Before an Old Painting of the Crucifixion

The Mission Carmel
June, 1960

I ponder how He died, despairing once.
I've heard the cry subside in vacant skies,
In clearings where no other was. Despair,
Which, in the vibrant wake of utterance,
Resides in desolate calm, preoccupies,
Though it is still. There is no solace there.

That calm inhabits wilderness, the sea,
And where no peace inheres but solitude;
Near death it most impends. It was for Him,
Absurd and public in His agony,
Inscrutably itself, nor misconstrued,
Nor metaphrased in art or pseudonym:

A vague contagion. Old, the mural fades . . .
Reminded of the fainter sea I scanned,
I recollect: How mute in constancy!
I could not leave the wall of palisades
Till cormorants returned my eyes on land.
The mural but implies eternity:

Not death, but silence after death is change.
Judean hills, the endless afternoon,
The farther groves and arbors seasonless
But fix the mind within the moment's range.
Where evening would obscure our sorrow soon,
There shines too much a sterile loveliness.

No imprecisions of commingled shade,
No shimmering deceptions of the sun,
Herein no semblances remark the cold
Unhindered swell of time, for time is stayed.
The Passion wanes into oblivion,
And time and timelessness confuse, I'm told.

These centuries removed from either fact
Have lain upon the critical expanse
And been of little consequence. The void
Is calendared in stone; the human act,
Outrageous, is in vain. The hours advance
Like flecks of foam borne landward and destroyed.

Angle of Geese

How shall we adorn
Recognition with our speech?—
  Now the dead firstborn
Will lag in the wake of words.

  Custom intervenes;
We are civil, something more:
  More than language means,
The mute presence mulls and marks.

  Almost of a mind,
We take measure of the loss;
  I am slow to find
The mere margin of repose.

  And one November
It was longer in the watch,
  As if forever,
Of the huge ancestral goose.

  So much symmetry!
Like the pale angle of time
  And eternity.
The great shape labored and fell.

  Quit of hope and hurt,
It held a motionless gaze,
  Wide of time, alert,
On the dark distant flurry.

ACKNOWLEDGEMENTS

Thomas Hardy, from *COLLECTED POEMS OF THOMAS HARDY*. Copyright © 1925 by The Macmillan Company. Reprinted by permission of the Trustees of the Hardy Estate and The Macmillan Company, New York, London and Collier-Macmillan Canada Ltd., Toronto.

Robert Bridges, from *POETICAL WORKS OF ROBERT BRIDGES*, 2nd edition. Copyright 1936 by Robert Bridges. Reprinted by permission of The Clarendon Press, Oxford.

Edwin Arlington Robinson, "Eros Turannos," "Veteran Sirens," and "The Wandering Jew," from *COLLECTED POEMS OF EDWIN ARLINGTON ROBINSON*. Copyright 1920 by Edwin Arlington Robinson, renewed 1948 by Ruth Nivison. Reprinted by permission of The Macmillan Company, New York. "Luke Havergal," from *THE CHILDREN OF THE NIGHT (1897)*. Reprinted by permission of Charles Scribner's Sons, New York.

T. Sturge Moore, from *THE POEMS OF THOMAS STURGE MOORE*, Collected Edition, Volume I, by permission of Miss H. H. R. Sturge Moore and Macmillan & Co., Ltd., London.

Adelaide Crapsey, from *VERSE*. Copyright 1922 by Algernon S. Crapsey, renewed by The Adelaide Crapsey Foundation. Reprinted by permission of Alfred A. Knopf, Inc., New York.

INDEX OF TITLES & FIRST LINES

---

*"A useless burden upon the earth," from Achilles' speech, *Iliad*, Book XVIII, line 104: "but I abide here by the ships a useless burden upon the earth."